# Writing
### as a Path to
# Awakening

# Writing
## as a Path to
# Awakening

### A YEAR TO BECOMING
### AN EXCELLENT WRITER AND
### LIVING AN AWAKENED LIFE

## Albert Flynn
## DeSilver

sounds true
BOULDER, COLORADO

Sounds True
Boulder, CO 80306

Published 2017

Cover design by Jennifer Miles
Book design by Beth Skelley

Cover image © Wisut Boonyasopit, shutterstock.com

"Poetic License" from *Collected Poems*, copyright © 2013 by Ron Padgett. Reprinted by
permission of Coffee House Press.

"Secrets" copyright © by Caroline Calhoun. Used with permission.

"Paris;this April sunset completely utters." Copyright © 1923, 1925, 1951, 1953, 1991 by
the Trustees for the E. E. Cummings Trust. Copyright © 1976 by George James Firmage,
from *Complete Poems: 1904–1962* by E. E. Cummings, edited by George J. Firmage. Used by
permission of Liveright Publishing Corporation.

"I Am Waiting" from *A Coney Island of the Mind*, copyright ©1958 by Lawrence Ferlinghetti.
Reprinted by permission of New Directions Publishing Corp.

"The Snow Man" from *The Collected Poems of Wallace Stevens*, copyright © 1954 by Wallace
Stevens and copyright renewed 1982 by Holly Stevens. Used with permission of Alfred
A. Knopf, an imprint of the Knopf Doubleday Publishing Group, a division of Penguin
Random House LLC. All rights reserved.

"Summertime Thing," copyright © 1997 Chuck Prophet and Mummyhead Music. Used with
permission.

Printed in Canada

Names: DeSilver, Albert Flynn, author.
Title: Writing as a path to awakening : a year to becoming an excellent
  writer and living an awakened life / Albert Flynn DeSilver.
Description: Boulder, CO : Sounds True, Inc., 2017.
Identifiers: LCCN 2016056604 (print) | LCCN 2017021640 (ebook) |
  ISBN 9781622039128 (ebook) | ISBN 9781622039111 (pbk.)
Subjects: LCSH: Authorship—Religious aspects. | Spiritual life. |
  Self-knowledge in literature.
Classification: LCC PN171.R45 (ebook) | LCC PN171.R45 D47 2017 (print) |
  DDC 808.02—dc23
LC record available at https://lccn.loc.gov/2016056604

10 9 8 7 6 5 4 3 2 1

This book is for all my "Writing as a Path to Awakening" students, past, present, and future. Thank you for your brilliant writing and creative geniusness, your support, courage, and inspiration!

To tap into your deepest talent, you need to seek out a calm, restful state of mind where your head isn't defending your delicate ego and your heart can bloom open a little.

**MARY KARR**

# Contents

# Acknowledgments

Thanks first and foremost to Loren Olds for the love and friendship, and for helping to complete the circle. And to Robert Lee for his excellence in editing and being—your support and belief in this book have been paramount! Thanks also to Haven Iverson, Christine Day, Tami Simon, and the rest of the crew at Sounds True.

With infinite love and gratitude always to Megan Freeman, teacher and guiding angel. To Karen Benke in love and friendship via writing, teaching, and being. And to my great "Writing as a Path to Awakening" primary venues, beginning with the mothership Spirit Rock, where it all began for me spiritually, emotionally, even poetically. Thanks to Jack Kornfield, Ajahn Jumnian, Heather Sundberg, Anna Douglas, and Anne Cushman especially. With thanks to the Omega Institute, Esalen Institute, and Shambhala Mountain Center. Thanks to Adayashanti and the many journeys of awakening through silence. To the late Bill Berkson who supported and encouraged and redirected my creative intentions toward poetry and writing. Thanks always to Todd Pickering, friend and bright creative catalyst. To the crew at TEDx Santa Cruz, who gave me the stage on which to clarify some of the core ideas for this book. To Cheryl Strayed and Elizabeth Gilbert, whose presence, creativity, and courage have been a perpetual guiding light. Thanks to Jennifer Urban Brown for your kind and generous help with the framework for this book. Thanks to all my friends, colleagues, and students at California Poets in the Schools. Though it has been a while, you are my eternal inspiration!

To Margaret and Serena with love and strength, and to the memory of Collette Ray Flynn and Carll Harrison DeSilver forever in love and gratitude. And to Marian, always with love.

# Premise, Promise, and Precepts

*I* would like to begin this book the same way I like to begin my workshops—by reminding everyone of their true nature via a very basic *premise*: You are enough. You are more than enough—you are a creative genius. And I'm not being nice, trying to endear you to me and my lovely little book here. This is basic original truth. Merely by the fact of your existence you can't help being a creative genius. This is your very nature; it's who you are—whatever your story or situation. You are constantly creating all the time. And yet like most of us, you might be creating from a familiar default set point of limited conditioning rather than from refined, unlimited open awareness. You might be a little out of alignment with the full force and flow of the universal creation energy that is you. Now is your time to realign your awareness and best intentions with that full creation energy. Take a deep breath, put your hand on your heart, and say it loud and proud (or if you are in a public location, loudly to yourself): *"I am a creative genius, I am a brilliant writer!"* Good. Welcome back. How does that feel?

Now being a creative genius and a brilliant writer doesn't necessarily mean that you are suddenly intellectually superior and advanced, particularly skilled, or even published. What it *does* mean is that by activating the truth of who you are in voice and body, you have begun to re-member and reactivate your full potential for all those things. It's just been dormant within you, waiting for the right time and the right catalyst to help set it free within you and the world. Let this book, this moment, be that reminding spark.

A brilliant writer is someone who is devoted to expressing their creativity through the written word. Devotion is the key. I like to say a writer is someone who writes, *not* someone who is published.

Practice, repetition, and consistency are essential. This book is designed to help you master all three. And because writing is not a separate activity from living, it's ultimately a book about Being with a cap*ital B*, about the integration of life and art.

*

The *promise*: If you read carefully and openly, truly give yourself to the practices in this book, tweaking them for your own development, and continue devotedly and consistently meditating, writing, reading, studying, attending live events (preferably one of mine), and letting go, you will become a more awake person and a better writer. It really is that simple in concept, and that challenging and rewarding in practice. In the meantime, happy reading! Enjoy the stories and have fun practicing the meditations and experimenting with the exercises. And if you gain something valuable from this book (or even if you don't—ha!), I sincerely hope to see you at some of my upcoming live workshops, retreats, or daylong intensives to help you integrate the material and further propel you along your path of creativity and awakening.

*

The *precepts*: Every great human spiritual tradition from around the world is structured around precepts in one way, shape, or form. From the most remote and obscure animistic hunter-gatherer cultures to the major Western religious traditions, humans have always sought grounding and connection in guidelines for behavior and action in regards to self, family, society, and the world at large. There is a reason such precepts and guidelines are common to virtually all cultures, religions, and integrated social units: they keep us connected, balanced, and engaged with community in a healthy, supportive way. I spent the first twenty-five years of my life disconnected, without any knowledge, understanding, or engagement with such a simple intentional framework—and it almost killed me. By following such an open and flexible code, we can stay grounded, motivated, and supported in our practices of creativity and spirituality. It's about keeping the collective safe and sane and rooting our highest spiritual and creative intentions in community support.

You can think of such precepts as an open moral code of conduct—the Eightfold Path of Buddhism, the Ten Commandments of Christianity, the principles of faith in Judaism, the codes of yogic discipline found in Hinduism, or the Five Pillars of Islam—but in a way free of the dogma and control that limits traditional religious frameworks. Yes, I too am suspicious of any patriarchal "morality police" commanding from up on high about how we should live and behave and in what context. For aboriginal cultures, morality codes come about more organically from ritual, storytelling, singing, and dancing, as expressed in action in relationship to an immediate landscape or place. Less doctrinal, more free-flow, which is what we're all about here.

In following a version of such precepts myself, I thought it relevant to tweak and orient them specifically to writing as a path to awakening, since this is not just a book about writing and creativity but also about *living* the awakened life. Again, this isn't some strict religious doctrine I insist you follow—quite the opposite. It's an *invitation* to enter this book in an open way, to enter your life in a newly expanded way yet with intentional healing parameters. Here are my ten precepts for writing (being) on the path to awakening. They ask us to commit to:

1. **Compassion for all living things.** Writing a successful novel requires presenting your central characters (be they protagonists or antagonists)—no matter how flawed, obnoxious, even murderous they are—with sympathy, empathy, and compassion. There is a difference between sympathy and empathy, and it starts with pity. Pity means acknowledging the suffering of others, but in a detached and even aloof way. Sympathy is a step up on the scale to feeling a sense of relatedness, of care and concern for someone else (or a fictional character) and their challenging situation. When we feel

empathy, however, we recognize and share in their emotional experience by seeing it from their perspective. In other words, empathy invites us to imagine ourselves *as* this person in their particular challenging situation, and feel it as they might feel it. Compassion exceeds even empathy. Compassion can be thought of as full emotional engagement with the other, as in suffering *with* them, where you experience little if any separation between you and the other person, animal, plant, or character. Their suffering is your suffering. It's a single universal, transcendently shared, emotional experience. This isn't always easy. Our social conditioning gears us toward separation and we inevitably experience conflicts with the people in our own family, community, and society. Yet cultivating compassion in writing creates a much more realistic, richly complex, and dynamically emotional experience for the reader (and, needless to say, you the writer). When such emotional depth is written into your characters, their stories become your story, both in fiction and in real life.

Writing is an expression of this basic embodied principle of holding a reverence for all life. Even though we realize there is suffering and delusion, inherent contradiction in ourselves and others—as with the mere fact that "life lives on lives" (the wild order of things in which animals kill and eat plants and other animals)—we still approach life and our creativity with patience, empathy, and compassion.

*

A quick word on suffering: Somewhere along the way, *dukkha*, the first of the Four Noble Truths in Buddhism, got translated as "all life is suffering." You hear people refer to this all the time. Let us set the record straight: it's not that all life *is* suffering, but rather that in life we experience suffering. It happens. Pain—emotional, mental, and physical—is part of the human condition. But here's the trick: the degree to which we suffer within that reality of pain is a *choice*.

Our relationship to that pain is everything. In Buddhism—primarily through the practice of meditation—we learn how to accept and live with suffering in a more open, compassionate, and forgiving way.

The words *delusion* and *illusion* also get recklessly thrown around and mixed up in spiritual circles. A delusion is a false belief about perception, experience, or reality itself. For example, we regularly believe that we are the name our parents gave us at birth, with a certain fixed personality, or that we *are* a persistent grating slew of emotions, or that we *are* merely a physical body. But these aspects are not the totality of who and what we truly are. More on this later. In contrast, an illusion is a deceptive sensory perception, where something seemingly real is actually a mistaken impression. Delusion and illusion go hand in hand. Most of us are *deluded* in our understanding about ourselves because of all the false *illusions* we have about what we see, think, and feel about ourselves. If the difference doesn't seem clear right now, please read on—I promise things will gel!

In commitment to this first precept, we act with intention toward sacred creativity, nonharming, and kindness toward ourselves and all living things in order to become more aligned with our full creative potential.

*

2. **Truth.** Writing is a path to accessing Truth with a capital *T* as well as a path for telling the truth with a lowercase *t*—the truths of our daily lives. We all noodle our way through life telling little white lies (often to ourselves first). It's usually just a matter of degree between what sets you and me apart from a blatant big old gnarly liar. Writing and mindfulness—when we truly commit to both practices—have a way of keeping us in check, keeping us scrupulous and honest. Meditation is a way of *being* truth. Writing is a medium for telling the truth.

3. **Not stealing.** Realizing there is infinite abundance, we see there is nothing to take from others and hoard for ourselves.

Pablo Picasso reportedly said, "Good artists copy; great artists steal." Twentieth-century poet and essayist T.S. Eliot expands on that for poets (and all writers) when he writes, "Immature poets imitate; mature poets steal." There is even a pop-creativity book out there by artist Austin Kleon that, as expressed in its title, encourages us to "steal like an artist." My interpretation of all this is that there is nothing new under the sun, that it is perfectly okay to imitate others when we are first starting out as a writer. As we evolve in our own creative process, we naturally assimilate much of what we read and study; we integrate it into the creation of our own voice and style. So go ahead—be creatively influenced. *Integrate* like an artist by blending and assimilating from the massive soup of creativity that has come before you, but *never, ever* copy or plagiarize.

4. **Merging with the one.** Sometimes this precept references the power of our sexuality and sexual energy as "right action." Generally used by consenting adults to consummate connection, amplify relationship, or make babies, our sexual energy—when used unwisely—can create deceit, great hurt, drama, and chaos in our personal lives. Sexual energy *is* our creative energy. Use it wisely, mindfully. Write from the body with kindness, awareness, compassion, and love.

5. **Nongrasping.** Write it down and let it go. Knowing there is an infinite wellspring of brilliant ideas, we let go of an ego that wants to overevaluate, take credit, define, grasp, and own the work.

6. **Purity.** Purity of intent, purity of practice, purity of body and mind. Attend to silence and to beauty, for these are your greatest sources of insight and creativity. Screen out toxic people, conflict-dependent media, and overtly

negative influences without denying suffering and
negativity's place in the world. Be conscious about what
you take into your body. Limit the harmful substances that
make you unconsciously (literally and figuratively) check
out, disconnect, avoid, or withdraw—be they certain
foods, drinks, or drugs (prescribed, illegal, or socially/
culturally accepted).

7. **Contentment.** Orient your mind (your life) toward the natural
   states of peace, ease, grace, compassion, and love. Doing so
   sets the ground for productivity and creativity.

8. **Burning enthusiasm.** Harness the energy of excitement and
   possibility—this is the creative energy of the universe. You are
   this energy; it's generated from within. Celebrate bright joy
   with your words and voice. It's positively contagious.

9. **Self-study.** Above my altar, where I sit in silence daily, I have
   a hand-painted and hand-printed work by the artist and
   publisher JB Bryan. It's a quote from the renowned thirteenth-
   century Zen master writer/poet Dogen:

To study the way
Is to study the self

To study the self
Is to forget the self

To forget the self
Is to be enlightened by all things

To be enlightened by all things
Is to remove the barrier
Between self and other.

> Now no trace of enlightenment
> Though enlightenment continues
> In daily life endlessly.

Self-reflection, self-inquiry, self-understanding. Find out who you *really* are through the practices of mindful reading, writing, deep meditation, and letting go of the small ego-self in order to enter into the reality of the boundless self.

10. **Celebrating the spiritual.** Celebrate your creativity and your very being in every moment, breath by breath, by practicing consistently on and off the cushion, on and off the page—in the depths of the gritty, inappropriate, shameful, freaky, contradictory, messy, violent, raging, beautiful life that is yours and yours alone. When writing is a spiritual act, your primary intent is unity consciousness.

**TRY THIS**  What are some values you live by? Do you have a sacred creed or follow certain precepts that guide your life? Write down your list now in order to explore and clarify this idea for yourself.

# Winter

# 1

# January
## {Rebirth}

*Introduction: Writing as a Path to Awakening*

*L*et's begin with a primal human question: *Who am I? Who am I, really?* "I cannot tell what I am, because words can describe only what I am not," said the twentieth-century Indian mystic Nisargadatta Maharaj in his book of conversations, *I Am That.*

We set off writing on the path to awakening by tuning into what we are not. "*Neti, neti,*" they say in India, "not this, not this." They say this as a process of negating that which is fleeting and untrue in order to access that which is divinely permanent and true. If we are not what words can describe, and words can describe pretty much everything in the physical/emotional universe, then what the heck are we? This is writing as a path to awakening's ultimate question, with the invitation to write and live your way into the answer.

Writing as a path to awakening is about how conscious living informs conscious writing (creativity) and, in turn, how conscious writing and creativity inform conscious living. It's one infinite loop—the helix of return. We begin with absences in January, in the "dead" of winter, burrowed inside our snow cave of the familiar, dreaming of courage to face the unknown, dreaming of transformation. We begin cold to our old story and become willing to let it go, aching to be reborn, willing to write our way into a new reality.

*

Speaking of old stories, and since throughout this book I will repeatedly ask you to be vulnerable and write into *your* own story, I figure I should set a good example right from the get-go. So here's an old story of mine.

I grew up in suburban Connecticut to distant and alcoholic parents who weren't really up for parenting, so they hired a governess named Miss Hedy. Remember Grendel from the epic poem *Beowulf*? That's Miss Hedy. She was a stubby monstrosity complete with chubby jowls, dark beady little eyes the color of a casket's shadow, and a head of mashed gray curls like tufts of ash. She wore a white starched nanny suit with vertical ribbed stripes that left imprints on my face when she pressed me to her giant bosom in a forced hug. If you could call that a hug. That was a rarity. Most of the time Miss Hedy barked commands and swatted at us, being strict, controlling, and eventually physically and emotionally abusive to my sisters and me. The only words I can remember coming from her mouth were "you should be ashamed of yourself." And for much of my life I was.

Between Mom's alcoholism, Dad's obliviousness, and Grendel's abuse, I started drinking at age twelve. By nineteen I was a committed binge drinker. There was a horrific night my freshman year of college where I was at a party with all my high school friends. I had just been recently dumped by my first college sweetheart. There were kegs; there was a kid in a trench coat wandering around with a bottle of Southern Comfort. I needed comforting. I drank far too many red plastic cups of keg beer and was riding the trench-coat coattails of Kid Southern Comfort. It wasn't long before I was stumbling around, spitting beer into people's breast pockets, asking for confirmation that they loved me (they clearly didn't), and generally making a complete ass of myself. I was finally chased from the house by the four hundredth person I had annoyed, and wound up staggering out into the driveway where I proceeded to black out face down on the asphalt. Nobody noticed I had gone, including my friend Mike, who at some point was done with the party and ready to drive home. He jumped into the car, cranked up Crosby, Stills, Nash, and Young (was it "Carry On" or "Helpless" bleeding through the floorboards?)—and backed right over me!

Somehow he heard me screaming. He stopped the car, dragged my bleeding body into his parents' yellow Jetta, and drove us both drunk to the hospital. The next morning Mom and Dad were there white-knuckling the bedrails and looking at me as if I'd just robbed a bank. They were disappointed. "Son, we're very disappointed in you," they said. More shame. More drinking. It was a cycle that continued until another hospitalization a couple years later in Colorado, when I was also arrested for assault and battery. I won't go into the details of that cheerful story here, but you can read all about it in my memoir, *Beamish Boy*.

At a certain point, with the law on one side and a girlfriend threatening to leave on the other (bless her heart), I finally quit drinking. I moved to California to start anew. I met a new friend who was in something called "therapy." He'd known me for all of one week when he said, "Dude, *you* need therapy." From my wounded and delusional viewpoint, he appeared to be fairly well-adjusted, so I joined his therapy group. Turned out his therapy group was really a psychedelic therapy *cult* and I got sucked into the madness. There were no boundaries—the teachers were using illegal drugs with their "students" and having sex with a select few. It was a mess—but not without some redeeming qualities (I will share one of my favorite stories from that experience at the end of the book). But suffice it to say, I "escaped" the group and soon found my way to meditation. I eventually drummed up the courage to participate in a silent meditation retreat, which turned out to be way more terrifying and challenging than being blindfolded, told to eat giant bowlfuls of psychedelic mushrooms, and spending the next eight hours vomiting and losing my mind.

It was just a couple years later, after I had left the group, and I was in my midtwenties when I found myself on one of my first silent retreats at Spirit Rock Meditation Center with the Thai meditation master Ajahn Jumnian. I had been struggling for days at the retreat, overwhelmed by the incessant chatter in my head—the constant evaluation, judgment, opinion, and projections—when I thought I literally might have to simply pack up and bolt. I'd fallen in love with several practitioners and imagined having mad, sprawling passionate sex with them in the pile of *zafus* at the back of the room. I'd labeled and judged the overweight people, ridiculed the skinny ones, pegged the lady with the blond hair and thick crimson makeup as a "trophy wife," became righteous about the whisperers who broke the noble silence, and cursed the control freaks at mealtime obsessing over their special diets. The commentator in my head was on a rampage from external to internal self-judgment and back, over and over again ad nauseam. "I'm a dumb-ass shitty writer," "I'm a mess," "I can't stay focused," "I'm so bored," "meditation is a stupid waste of time," "I'm outta here," "I'm a racist, a sexist, a classist, an ageist," "I'll never complete a book," "why am I such a judgmental asshole?" etc. At a certain point, I couldn't help to wonder: Was I always this judgmental? Where was all this judgment coming from?

After lunch on the fourth day I wandered off into the woods to do some lying-down meditation and hopefully fall asleep and make all this internal torment go away. I hiked into the small canyon and found a perfect flat spot of clean sand in the middle of a dry creek bed; I lay down and closed my eyes. I began by following my breath and then tried one of Ajahn's body scans he had taught us the day before. I was drifting off into a deep and spacious meditative zone when my mind (and body) were overtaken by what I can only describe as a vision. It was similar to a spectacularly vivid dream at night, in which you wake up screaming or sweating, or at the very least are freaked out for days afterward because of the intense "reality" of it. The weird thing was, I was awake but clearly in an altered state of awareness after days of intensive meditation. It was not unlike one of the psychedelic "medicine journeys" with mushrooms I had done in the therapy cult, but without the side effects of nausea, vomiting, terror, and intense dread.

I find myself transported back in time to 1973 to the cold, tiled, downstairs hallway just outside the bedroom of my childhood home in Connecticut, which we called the Clock Tower in honor of the large clock adorning its Georgian façade. I'm four or five years old. Grendel, our vicious governess, is there. Her eyes are full of rage; venom is in her voice. She's wearing a blue nightgown—torn, frayed, and full of holes. Instead of skin underneath that threadbare cloth I see tiny points of light and what appears to be smoke spilling through the tatters. The hallway is dark and hazy. Miss Hedy screams at me, in some kind of apoplectic state, to pick up my clothes. She is ranting in a demonic German tongue. I can't understand what she's saying; it's just pure, garbled rage. It's as if all the words have gotten sliced into incoherent pieces on the rusty blade of her tongue and have shattered all around me. The sound is making my rib cage rattle.

Suddenly, she lunges at me and grabs my arm to show me what an incredible mess I've created. She yanks me into the pile of clothes, trying to push my face in it like she did with my cat, Snowy, that time he peed in my bedroom closet. But my arm breaks off in her hand. More frustrated than shocked, she throws it aside, blood spewing, like a cheap mop handle. Then she grabs my ear, which comes off in her grasp, peeled from my head with a slurping sound, and she tosses it aside like a grapefruit rind. Then she goes for my hair, tufts of it filling her sweaty palms as if she's pulling dead weeds. She attacks my other limbs, each time filled with a more virulent rage, until I'm reduced to a ragged, limbless stump. I'm just wobbling there—torn and bloody, utterly useless to her. She expands and bloats, turning from a fuming red to a dark purple, bursting the seams of her tattered nightgown. Suddenly, she explodes. And just like that, she vaporizes into a puff of pale blue smoke. She is cast into the Outer Void, beyond this world, and I am jarred awake.

I sat up in the creek bed, feeling the earth beneath me as if for the very first time; the air was crackling with the electricity of liberation. I was filled with a sensation of absolute release. A profound wave of freedom and complete relief overtook me—my body bright with the weight of sunlight. I grabbed onto a couple of large rocks to keep my body from drifting up into the canopy of trees. I found myself sobbing into the riverbed, the tears of a thousand lifetimes. I was convinced I'd just experienced an exorcism of sorts—something dark and metallic, horrific and sticky, had been ejected from my body, and along with it my story of abuse and abandonment, neglect and disconnection. That narrative of illusions burned up in the roiling blue smoke with Miss Hedy. And I realized in both body and mind that in some sense I'd been reborn. I was definitely *not* my story.

*

Back to that primal human question: Who am I? Am I this list of experiences, these memories of my childhood and young adulthood? Am I these feelings and emotions associated with those memories? Am I my opinions and beliefs? Am I even this flesh-and-bone body that will grow old and die? These are all examples of what words can describe. Remember what Maharaj says: "I cannot tell what I am, because words can describe only what I am not."

What I discovered is that *I am that which makes language possible*—that which makes stories possible, that which makes joy, hope, and love possible; writing and poetry possible; that which makes all emotion and compassion possible. This is who we really are, who *you* really are—an open, poetic, living, breathing language-body of possibility! You are not your story; you are a field of possibility ready to be reborn!

> **TRY THIS**   What are the core transformative events of your life? I'm talking about the events that shaped your evolution as a character, a person—overtly dramatic events or intimate and quiet moments (something your father said that you never forgot) that shaped your very being. Write down a list of at least five major moments in your own life that shook you, emotionally and spiritually, to your core—events that signal points of transformation or rebirth in your life's narrative.

## ON AWAKENING

The word *awakening* probably conjures up all sorts of images in your mind. Like with the words *nirvana* and *enlightenment*, we imagine peaceful sages filled with profound wisdom, wearing goldenrod-colored robes, wreaths of marigolds around their necks. Maybe you also imagine flowing gray beards spilling down their skinny chests, exotic locks rivering down their backs. Or maybe they have brightly shaved heads, eyes glowing in cosmic reverie or closed in sublime contemplation as they perch on thrones, cushions, the dirt floors of austere caves. Perhaps they sit before thousands of adoring fans who have not yet achieved the profound state of (and usually *his*) eternal bliss. Our fantasy of an awakened person usually doesn't look like us. They don't wear our clothes, don't come from our culture, and don't possess our level of commitment to the spiritual path (assuming most of us have not chosen to live as ascetic monastics). Thank god they're just projections of our minds!

I believe there are three basic evolutionary steps of awakening consciousness. Broken down, they look like this:

**Step 1   The concept of awakening.** The first step is the *idea* of awakening. This idea includes everything that we think of as awakening or enlightenment—all the images, thoughts, and feelings we conjure up around the concept from what we've read, heard, and seen on TV and the Internet. This idea also includes any accumulated knowledge we might have about awakening, whether we read a snippet on a blog post somewhere or have been studying ancient texts for the last fifty years. Our idea of awakening is an essential first step: it engages us and draws us into a greater possibility for our heart and mind. It reminds us that we can be more expansive and inclusive in our sense of self. However, our idea of awakening is merely cursory.

**Step 2   The energy of awakening.** The second step of awakening occurs when we have an intense experience during yoga, meditation, chanting, or an extended period of silence. In this step, we actually feel a sensory experience of awakening in our body, wherein we release layers of emotional tension, grief, fear, longing, doubt, and anxiety. We might experience profound bodily sensations of shaking, tingling, floating, and even detaching from our body altogether. Some people describe this as bursts of kundalini energy shooting through the body, opening us up to clear, peaceful, and blissed-out states of awareness that can last minutes, days, or even years. Not to belittle or underestimate their profundity, but ultimately these physical states dissipate and change. We eventually return to our body, to familiar mind-states and changing moods.

**Step 3 Full surrender.** The third evolutionary step of awakening happens when we completely surrender—we let go beyond thought, body, and experience itself. This nonexperience is what yogis refer to as the *deathless state*—the state of pure consciousness, pure potentiality. There are few living embodied examples of this state and it's virtually impossible to talk about because it can't be described with words. However, as mentioned before, this state *makes* language possible, makes experience possible, makes consciousness itself possible. Someone embodying such a state reflects back a steady stream of light and love. When you're in the presence of someone like this, you never feel any resistance, ego, agenda, or need—this is a being whose soul intent is to radiate pure clarity, compassion, and joy.

When I use the word *awakening* in this book, I mostly mean the development of mindfulness, the evolutionary process of expanding consciousness, and *not* a perfected static state of bliss. We are "perfect" in every moment, in every stage of our lives—in our grief and anger as well as in our excitement and joy. Part of what makes us truly human are our foibles and mistakes along the path of an evolutionary enlightenment. This is where communication comes in—how we speak or write forth our experiences in infinitely varied ways is endlessly fascinating to me.

What I have personally discovered is that there is no "getting there"—we are "there" at every moment, though we may feel that we are *more* "there" at certain times than others. All experience is spiritual experience, and for me that especially holds true for the writing experience. That's the simple message of this book. When we wake up to that simple truth, we become awakened in our creativity and in each aspect of our daily lives. I'm not just saying this to let you off the hook easily.

We still have to show up fully and take responsibility for our emotional responses, all the while remembering that this whole conundrum is an evolutionary practice. We are opening up in stages depending on how willing and available we are to the process of surrendering to the mystery of awareness in any given moment.

Many people have spiritual experiences at different times in their lives. Often people describe being filled with light or feeling charged with divine energy. They report feeling an infinite permeability, merging with the holy, becoming infused with an "unbearable lightness of being," to quote the great Czech writer Milan Kundera. Some people recount the sensation of leaving their bodies, floating up to the ceiling or sky. Some people relate near-death or full-death experiences with eventual returns to embodiment. These episodes can also happen during periods of profound grief or depression, in dreams, under extreme physical duress, or at moments of severe injury. They can occur during energetically charged situations, during intense sexual experiences, while giving birth, or while witnessing a birth. They can take place after days of being in silent retreat at a Zen center, or singing Christian hymns, or participating in a Sufi dance, or gathering with others in Jewish prayer. They can happen at a Lakota Sun Dance, while out on a solo backpacking journey, or at a Grateful Dead (or pick your favorite band) concert. They can occur while skydiving, skiing, or swimming with the dolphins; while doing psychedelics at a session in "therapy" (see my book *Beamish Boy* for more on this), after reading a great poem, or while taking the bus to work. But what all these examples have in common is that they are *experiences*, which means they are temporary.

I don't want to minimize the importance or profundity of these experiences; rather, I want to highlight the fact that we are not our experiences—we are that which makes the experiences possible. It is so easy for our minds to interpret such occurrences as "the real deal," as some ongoing kind of truth, but they are merely fleeting. The human mind grabs on and attaches to them because of the physical/emotional surge in awareness—we feel incredible, we feel alive and connected, transported to a higher level of consciousness! So we connect to spirit, but then we come back down. The concert is over. We've had our orgasm. Now we have to feed the kids, deal with their tantrums, and put them through college. The sun goes down and we get cold and hungry. Eventually we have to return to work, and we're back in our head navigating our daily life, stumbling around in the cathedral of the mundane and ordinary, right where we started.

The challenge is how to integrate such transcendent experiences into our daily life, so we don't forget who we really are: that essence of connected free spirit. And yet it's not that we're seeking to "get back there," wherever "there" is, or to repeat a blissful adventure, but rather to become more aware in our daily life, to become more awake right now. It is important to remember that all reality is divine reality. There is a physical component to our experiences that is as divine as any ethereal mystical reality we might feel in heightened states. It's really a question of integration and balance. And one of the best ways I've found to integrate such experiences is through the practice of writing.

The following chapters include exercises and practices to help you integrate and balance daily life mind with divine creativity mind. In each chapter, I've placed the meditation exercises first, because I always suggest beginning with the meditation as a point of intention, even as a point of prayer for receiving and generating poetic (writing) ideas. Have fun with these exercises—experiment and play. This book is intended to be a practical and inspirational guide to further inspire your writing and being along this magical path to awakening we call life.

## ON WRITING

The practice of writing is an exploration of consciousness, a practice toward deeper self-awareness that moves us along the path of awakening to our true nature. The most profound spiritual teachers from around the world are often writers. From Sappho in the seventh century BCE to Pema Chödrön today, from Rumi in the thirteenth century, to Thomas Merton, Jack Kornfield, and the Dalai Lama, the written word has the power not only to inspire but also to awaken the very best in the human heart.

Writing as a path to awakening begs the question: Awakening to *what?* Again, awakening means waking up from the dream of separation. It means waking up from identifying with our stories, thoughts, opinions, and beliefs, and seeing beyond our knee-jerk emotional responses. Some of these habitual responses come from long-established patterns of conditioning, hurt, and trauma that have accumulated within us throughout the course of our lives. Writing as a path to awakening asks you to turn your attention inward toward the wisdom of a poetically open heart and mind, and away from an exclusive entanglement with the clutches of external physicality. This concept and process asks you to take time and gain perspective by watching the inscrutable play of thought. The practice involves witnessing the mind in action, doing its wild and zany dance—choosing in the moment not to react, but instead continuing to sit with eyes closed, breathing into your body with a commitment to patience, peace, insight, and surrender.

Writing is one of the most powerful points of focus we have as human beings. Writing is an act of creation, as speaking is an act of creation. It's the impulse—the catalyst that takes an idea from the mind and launches it on its journey into physical reality on the page. Writing is transformational; it has the power to transmit amorphous pulsations of thought-energy into concrete ideas through empty space. To paraphrase Stephen King, writing is telepathy. Pure and simple. I can set a detailed image in my head to words—written down, printed on paper, published in a book, and read by someone thousands of miles away, and they can see that image in their own mind's eye, thereby experiencing the emotional intent of it. Now that's magic. Writing is an act of magic, a catalyst for manifestation. Now, of course, not all words are created equal—not all sentences, paragraphs, or stories have the same effect. Some are imbued with more catalytic power, more transformational impact than others. And few of us are born with the gift of being able to string along words symphonically with apparent ease. Most of us must practice the craft, study the masters, repeatedly hash it out on the page, read and reread, fail and refail, play and play on, then practice some more. Practice in writing doesn't make perfect. Practice makes process. And if you can get yourself to practice enough, to the point of creating and then engaging in a consistent process, it will turn into a habit, a routine, and then you are on your way to success.

This book is designed to inspire you to do just that through anecdote and illumination, via innovative writing exercises designed to habituate you toward a daily writing practice. Writing and sitting meditation practices are a powerful pair, a dynamic duo—think Thelma and Louise, Batman and Robin, Lewis and Clark, Laverne and Shirley, or Candace and Toni (from *Portlandia*). Together they nourish and push, trigger and define, inform and inspire, enable and energize. To engage in both practices fully is to activate a more complete creative and spiritual self. The invitation is here and now; your time to be reborn is this instant. Take time to breathe in silence and surrender to your innate creative genius! Then go forth, wake up, and write!

*

So far we have set off on our creative journey with our premise, promise, and precepts along with an invitation in chapter 1 to wake up and be reborn to our innate creative genius. In chapter 2 we move on to "becoming through reading"—that is, using reading to become a stronger writer. I've written the chapters progressively to have a cumulative effect in order, month by month, so that by the end of the year you have the experience of having been through a complete evolutionary creative cycle, newly inspired and enthusiastically motivated. Have fun exploring the following meditation first, followed by the writing exercise. This will calm, settle, open, and prepare your mind for further insight and revelation in your reading, your writing, and your life.

### An Introductory Meditation

There is a big difference between mindfulness—focused attention or awareness to your immediate experience—and a cultivated meditation practice. Although you'll find different meditation exercises throughout this book, I highly recommend meeting with a trained meditation instructor and working with them to develop your practice (again, I hope you will consider joining me at upcoming live events, retreats, or workshops). Mindfulness is a simple shift of awareness—from being lost in thought, distracted, and spacing out, to noticing that you are lost in thought. This is a subtle yet profound point of attention. What I'm calling meditation, however, refers to stringing along a series of these points of attention in a more continuous flow toward deeper internal awareness. It's an intentional dedicated and engaged practice of settling the mind and body in a structured format, usually grounded in a particular physical position (standing, walking, sitting, or lying down) for a minimum time period, where we repeatedly bring our conscious attention back to the breathing body, by reciting mantras (uplifting or positive sacred phrases) or turning our awareness to internal physical sensations, emotions, and mind-states. Usually it's some combination of these practices. In this type of meditation, we don't fixate on any particular goal, attainment, personal improvement, better mind-state, or enhanced anything about our body and mind. We simply allow things to be as they are.

Easier said than done. Let's give it a try. Or another try, for those of you who have been meditating for years.

Find a comfortable and quiet place to sit. Sit upright so that you won't fall asleep, but comfortably. Close your eyes gently and rest your hands easily in your lap. Take off your shoes and rest your feet flat on the floor.

Begin by taking a single deep breath inward and exhale slowly. Take another deep breath and exhale slowly. Take a third. Keep your eyes closed gently, breathe regularly, and just tune into the rhythm of your breathing. Feel your body relaxing into the chair or cushion. If you feel obvious points of tension, breathe into those points and let them relax. Let your shoulders drop, loosen any tightness in your neck, and just relax into the chair, allowing your breath to be calm and natural. Breathe in, breathe out. You might bring your attention to where you feel the breath moving in your body—is it in the rise and fall of your chest or belly? Maybe in the wisps of air at your nostrils?

Breathe in, breathe out. Know in this moment that there is nothing to do, no knowledge to gather or remember, no proper way to breathe, nothing to get right or control. Just sit and notice the experience of your breathing body, letting all tension and expectations go. There is no right or wrong, nothing to accomplish or learn, nothing to figure out or fix. Just allow everything to be as it is. Breathe in, breathe out. Allow your mind to rest in an open state. Let thoughts be thoughts, sensations be sensations. Just rest here breathing through all that arises in heart and mind with full awareness, allowing yourself to feel bathed in silence, attuned to the reality of the present moment, breath by breath.

After a few minutes you might get caught on a train of thought toward planning or remembering, and when you notice this, simply come back to your experience of your breathing body. Breathe in, breathe out.

Continue to sit in silence following your breath for as little as ten or as much as sixty minutes. In a minute you will hear the sound of a bell (on the audio). At this point you can return to your breathing body and continue in silence for as long as you want and ring your own bell to close the meditation session, or take a deep breath and open your eyes now to complete the meditation.

———◆◆◆———

Feel free to use the guided meditations throughout this book as open contemplation time that enables you to let go and loosen up your creative energies, or as a springboard into some of the writing exercises. An extremely powerful practice is to come straight out of meditation and into writing practice, either with a spontaneous freewrite or by engaging in a more extended writing session.

### ➤ *An Introductory Writing Exercise*

Much has been written about freewriting and stream-of-consciousness writing, so I won't go into them in depth here other than to say that they have been the two most helpful and productive aspects of my writing practice. Most people would consider freewriting and stream-of-consciousness writing to be the same thing. I understand them to be distinct in that freewriting or freewrites are framed by a specific amount of time, as an exercise and practice. Stream-of-consciousness writing is continuous free association, unbound by time frame or length. Think Jack Kerouac's *On the Road* or the uncensored journals of Anais Nin. I have noticed that the more I practice truly letting go and getting out of my own way, the more raw, honest, insightful, and revealing my writing becomes. Our minds are so quick to judge and condemn, to interfere and sabotage—to self-censor—that much of the time we don't even know it's happening. The mind moves faster than we realize. A judgment about the practice of freewriting and whether or not it works for you has already shaped your perception and turned it into a belief before you can shut off your mind for long enough to even get some words down on paper.

I have a strict no cell phone policy for all my extended "Writing as a Path to Awakening" retreats, to give participants an opportunity to truly unplug. A couple years ago I had a student who kept pulling out her cell phone during writing sessions after multiple requests to put it away. She insisted that this was the way she wrote—the only way she could write. She claimed the speed at which she could type on her phone outpaced the speed at which her doubting self-sabotaging mind could interfere and shut her down. During the writing periods, she appeared to be texting her friend while everyone else toiled away by hand in their paper notebooks. I was skeptical, but open. After the third writing session or so, she raised her hand to share. She read direct from her phone as if she were sharing an intimate text exchange. The writing was fantastic. Raw and immediate, filled with a seething passion and vulnerability. She won me over. My no cell phone policy has since been amended.

Sometimes freewriting is frustrating and clunky. You don't get down what you hoped to get down, in the way you wanted it to come out. But the point is you got it out. So tough beans. Freewriting isn't your time for brilliance; it's your time for productivity. Keep going. Press on against the resistance, doubt, and judgment. After twenty minutes try again. Go for a walk and come back an hour later. Try again at night, after a meal, a cup of tea or coffee.

Write when you don't want to—that's often when the most real and revelatory material surfaces. The practice of writing (or anything, for that matter) isn't about wanting or not wanting to do it; it's about doing the work you've been called to do, the work you are committed to do. You don't second-guess feeding your child, even when you're fried, chronically annoyed, and ready to strangle the little angel. The same thing applies here. Don't ask yourself if you're in the mood to write or if you feel inspired. These are fleeting and irrelevant feelings for a writer to dwell in. In our mind we think that happiness is predicated on doing what we want or like to do in any given instant, but studies show over and over again that true lasting joy-in-your-soul happiness comes from generosity, from giving to and helping others, and from a feeling of competence generated by fulfilling a commitment—that is, following projects through to completion. The more we write through resistance and the more we write through the times we don't want to write, the less pull resistance and distraction will have on us, the more confidence we build, and the more likely we are to finish that writing project.

The practice is simple. Set a timer. Begin with a short time period (say, five minutes) and build up to longer periods of time. Then, follow a specific prompt. Write with no agenda and no concern for punctuation, grammar, spelling, or proper sentence structure. Allow yourself to write what is right there within you in the moment. Write quickly and urgently, letting the words fall out and onto the page without stopping to correct, modify, manipulate, or edit. You don't have to show this to anyone, so you are free to write simply and directly from the heart. Allow yourself to write crap! Experiment, try it, and see for yourself what arises. Have fun, stay with it, and over time you will experience your own beauty and creativity reawakening within you.

Here's a useful prompt to start you off: Freewrite for five minutes about something being born. You can take this as literally or metaphorically as you wish—witnessing the birth of a human or animal, or the birth of an idea, dream, hope, or insight. Don't think too much about it. Put your pen to paper or your fingers to the keyboard and go!

# 2

# February
## {Becoming}

### *Reading on the Path to Awakening*

Here's a funny question: What is reading? I mean *really*. The act of looking at words splayed across a page or screen? (An army of ants skittering across an expanse of white sand, a flock of geese strewn windward against a dusk-lit sky.) Maybe reading is a primal act of tracking and hunting. Footprints, deer trails, wing movements in the batted-down brush. We are looking for signs of movement, action, food. Contemporary reading is based on an ancient primal embodied knowledge of studying the landscape—scrawl of branches against a winter sky, tide patterns left in the sand at the tip of the ocean's reach, a musical script the wind left via quick ripples against the calm face of the bay, hexagonal patterns of drought-cracked earth, debris patterns at flood lines, terminal moraines and glacial erratics (giant stones left behind in open meadows by receding glaciers). Each a lone word, sentence, phrase, or paragraph—nature leaves her book wide open, her journal pages flapping in the wind, for us to drink in by reading. Nature is always writing her song for us to read and to sing.

Every time you step outside, you join the conversation started by the earth. Every time you crack open a book and set out on the hunt for original knowledge, the conversation expands. The more deeply you read and the more attention you offer, the more will be revealed to and through you. You are becoming both a sponge and a catalyst for new ideas. A good reader is also a mirror, springboard, ping pong, tree, or celestial object casting forth a beam of light or shadow. You are taking in others' ideas—tasting, contemplating, digesting, and making them your own. When you read deeply, you inhabit another dimension of reality, engaging in an act of creation initiated by the writer. It's as if the writer set off on the hunting expedition. Having broken trail, batted down the brush, and recorded their sightings, they now invite you along, pointing you in a new direction, handing you the map of pages and a string of crumbs (words) to follow into the vast wilderness of your imagination. When your imagination is triggered, you get inspired to reflect and generate. Good writing teleports you into new and revelatory places (landscapes), time periods, psychologies, emotional states, and even spatial dimensions. The sprawl of black script marching across the page or the digital zeros and ones arriving on the screen pulsate as thought assembled in a particular sequence, as a narrative in order to convey an idea. It starts as an invitation and then grows (depending on the reader's level of commitment) as a bond between writer and reader. It's an act of convergence between two seemingly distant strangers, a way of linking humanity, bridging the illusory chasm between us.

*

February is the ultimate time for reading, snuggled as we are in the heart of winter. We have spent the past couple of months turning inward, delving deep within, hibernating, growing our hunger for knowledge and self-awareness—gestating, digesting—slowly but surely becoming by gathering, absorbing, and *being* with language. We read as an act of reflection, for the respark of discovery and wonder; we read as an act of becoming who we really are.

Two of my most profound early reading experiences were Roald Dahl's *Danny, the Champion of the World* and S. E. Hinton's *The Outsiders.*

After *Charlotte's Web, Danny, the Champion of the World* was the first reading experience that transported me to another dimension and another reality. For the first time, I recognized this reality as the depths of my own imagination. As readers, we often give all creative credit to the writer, when in fact it's a collaborative experience. What I remember most about the experience of reading *Danny* was the imagery, and how my mind (inspired by Dahl's words) took me away from the loneliness and pain of my troubled alcoholic adolescence and straight into a magical forest in England. It wasn't so much the plot—Danny saving the pheasants and the triumph of good over evil. What got me was the power of Dahl's words, his ability to lead me into another world and how that sparked the potential of my own mind. His was a richly imagined world of dark forests; a dreamy, albeit cramped, caravan; intricately colored pheasants; and a world filled with adventure, fun, beauty, excitement, and danger. It was an imaginary place made completely real for a time in my mind, as real as any place that existed or could exist in reality. It awakened within me a sense of participatory possibility—a sort of invitation embroidered into an unspoken agreement of collaboration. The writer's attention goes into crafting language in a highly particular way in order to communicate on a deep level with the reader. The more the reader invests in that experience of being with each word and sentence, the more they enter into the world of that story and are thereby taken by it and given access to the emotional intent of the writer. Meanwhile, the reader's own imagination and emotional experience activates. Reading is an active, immersive process. Because of my eyesight challenges (strabismus), I have always been a slow and repetitive reader, which has actually helped me as a writer. If all writing is rewriting, then all reading is rereading, especially if you are a writer. The two are inextricably connected and necessary for the growth of the other. To become a better reader, write. To become a better writer, read. If you happen to read purely for entertainment's sake, by all means, move quickly, skim, flip pages, or gloss over. But if you want to be a better scholar or writer, slow down, go deep, and reread.

As I noted above, *The Outsiders* also had a formative effect on my early reading. The book revolves around the conflict between rival groups of kids—the Greasers and the Socials—in 1960s Tulsa, Oklahoma. It's a classic coming-of-age story told from the perspective of the protagonist, Ponyboy Curtis. The characters fight over territory and girlfriends, resulting in unintended murders, revenge, loss, and redemption. Great stuff! As a kid growing up in 1970s suburbia, I could still very much identify with the socioeconomic divides described in the book (even though New Canaan, Connecticut, was vastly different than 1960s Tulsa, Oklahoma). Personally, I identified with both groups: although I could have been considered a Social, I hung out with a lot of Greasers.

That whole world of the gang—the socialization, the adventure and danger, the smoking and drinking—that's what I grew up with. My mother was a devout socialite, an alcoholic, and a big smoker. With two older sisters, I was barred from their girl games and left to my own devices, which meant spending a lot of time alone. By the time I was in high school, I was sick of it. I craved a gang. I jumped into a fun and adventurous social life with a diverse group of friends that revolved mostly around exploring our sexuality, smoking, and drinking. It eventually drew me into one of the greatest social party experiments ever—the Grateful Dead. Deadheads were all about rejecting conventional society and Nancy Reagan's "Just Say No" America. Our obvious reply? *Just say yes*, and with a defiant vengeance. I saw myself swimming in an exciting current of creative outsiders, until I grew up and out of it (and the Dead went mainstream).

*The Outsiders* sparked my imagination, inspired me, and triggered my emotions. I felt captivated by these people who didn't actually exist. And I recognized the power in that book as a form of magic. Ponyboy, Soda, Dallas, Darry, Cherry . . . these characters were as real to me in some ways as my own friends (Keith, Khan, Pietro, Pat, Jessica, Kathy, and Dawn). We hung out, smoked and drank, had flings and fiery romances, and even got in drunken fights (with each other). Thankfully, we didn't commit any murders or set any fires. Even so, we experienced plenty of hurt, deceit, and self-destruction.

I haven't thought about that book much at all in the past forty years, and yet here I am writing about my experience of it. Until recently, I didn't realize how immersive and profound that reading experience was—and now, a coming-of-age gang story features prominently in my latest novel.

Only in retrospect can I truly appreciate the effect those books had on me at a young age. I remember being thoroughly swept away by those S. E. Hinton novels, feeling so excited to reconnect with my "friends" on the page, eager to find out what happened to them—if they would (or would not) make it through. It was liberating, even healing, to be transported to a different emotional reality, as I was subconsciously eager to escape the abusive and neglectful aspects of my own.

Until I reread the synopsis of *The Outsiders*, I didn't remember the important role that poetry plays in the turning point of the novel. After an accidental murder when the boys are hiding from the law and our hero, Ponyboy, tries to soothe Johnny (who is on the run), he reads Johnny a poem by Robert Frost that ends with:

> So dawn goes down to day.
> Nothing gold can stay.

That Hinton had a sensibility for poetry and read it throughout her teen years, subsequently weaving it into her novel, says a lot about the power of reading and its potential influence on one's writing. This poem is a poem of awakening to the fleeting nature of experience—of words, ideas, images, stories, and even life itself. It's about being present to the beauty of the moment. Reading this poem anchors us to the emotional power of the story; that's the essence of reading on the path to awakening.

> **TRY THIS**   Now it's your turn. What were the formative reading experiences of your childhood? How have they informed your sensibility or interest in writing, and why? Take a few minutes to write down a short list of books or stories and what you loved about reading them.

Let's consider reading as something that happens on three primary levels:

1. **The skim.** You skim the surface, lazily dragging your net full of holes along the top of the lake, letting escape brilliant slivers of light. You are gliding, trawling for surface florals—little bright flowers you appreciate for a moment and then discard for the next one. As bubbles rise to the surface, they catch the light ever so briefly. Perhaps a rainbow appears and then dissolves back into invisibility, leading to a quick insight or uplift. Hopefully, it's enough to inspire a deeper plunge.

2. **The swim.** On this level of reading, you actually get wet—that is, you hunker down with a text by actively taking in most of the pages. You put your face in the water and allow yourself to be affected by the action, characters, and overall content. The plot makes you curious; the characters inspire your interest and care. You take a dip in a kelp forest and marvel at the unexpected diversity of fishes, enjoying them for a while before letting it all go. Then you move on to the next book.

3. **Submersion.** On this level of reading, you put on your diving suit and oxygen tank and go deep. You get sucked quickly beneath the surface and feel eager to plumb the depths. The pressure builds as you descend. You feel so engaged with the text that you want to reread passages to yourself, or read them aloud to others. You get physical with the book: You carry it lovingly around in your purse or bag as you might a small dog. You pet the cover, massage the spine, fondle the pages. You prattle on to random strangers about how they *need* to read it, in the way one needs to stay well hydrated or make regular visits to the dentist. And you get a bit possessive (maybe only a little when it comes to books), won't let anyone borrow it. "I'll buy you a copy," you say. You highlight certain passages and dog-ear pages; you write notes in the margins or in a separate notebook. The book jolts your mind into new modes of thinking and feeling; it moves you to appreciation or even to action. In other words, at this layer of reading you go from passively consuming to participating to co-creating.

Moving from consumer to participant-creator can only happen when you actively engage a text. Most people simply skim a book. Fewer people actively read and go deeper to understanding and inspiration. An even smaller percentage gets physical with the book by underlining, rereading, reading out loud, rewriting, reflecting, and taking notes. Through this process, these people may feel moved to create on their own; they realize they have something to say, something to contribute. Now they feel ready to lead the diving expedition! Maybe they find little gaps in stories that need filling in, or they want to right a wrong, or they hear a character expressing something left unsaid in the story they just finished. Regardless, these people see an opening for their own voice.

Some people like to experience books through audio. Great. But keep in mind that there is a difference between passive listening and active engagement. I invite you to dive deep: take notes, replay passages, recite them aloud, and get inspired to write forth your truth!

*

I was never a great student, and my first year of college was a glaring example of that. Since I didn't get into the University of Vermont, Hobart, or St. Lawrence, I ended up at a small college in Ohio my mother might have referred to as "East Jesus U." The College of Wooster turned out to be a good school, but I spent most of my time brooding and drinking, missing my friends on the East Coast, wondering what I was doing in Ohio. My roommate was a consummate Deadhead, which I loved at the time (although heavy drinking, drug use, and frequent road trips to Dead shows across the country took their toll). He had an awesome tape collection (cassette tapes, that is—way before CDs and MP3s) and cool tapestries. Plus, he was a gifted talker and seemed smart and interesting when he wasn't doing bong hits (and later, heroin). We took a couple of classes together. He rarely seemed to complete the reading or homework and yet always aced the tests. I consistently bailed on the reading and homework and regularly failed the tests. Despite that difference, his influence on me was notable.

In our second semester, we were assigned to read Sherwood Anderson's *Winesburg, Ohio* in American Lit. As it turned out, the real Winesburg, Ohio, was not too far from where we were in Wooster. I can't remember if we were required to go there for the class or if it was Mike's idea for a mini road trip. Regardless, it involved our regular departure ritual of hitting Daryl's Drive-Thru Liquor (conveniently located at the foot of campus) for a twelve-pack of Milwaukee's Best. And then off we went to do a little hands-on research, even though Anderson's book was based on a different town entirely (Clyde, Ohio, up near Lake Erie). Consequently, we both became surprisingly interested in the book. It's more of a cycle of short stories than a novel, and it revolves around the chronic isolation and dissatisfaction of the inhabitants of a small Ohio town. It also illustrates their chronic judgments and misperceptions of themselves and each other, which is all compounded by their inability (lack of awareness, unwillingness?) to communicate their feelings.

In a rare burst of enthusiasm, we not only read the book but also reread certain passages, underlined others, and discussed the themes and characters to help us prepare for class discussions. As I noted above, this level of study was uncharacteristic of me. My roommate and I came back from Winesburg with some interesting factoids about the actual town and how it related to Anderson's portrayal. For example, after European settlers displaced the Native people to reservations out west, the town was originally called Weinsberg after the German "founders." The Weinsberg family wanted to open a college in the area, but their house burned up in a fire—all their money, deeds, and important papers needed for founding the school went up in smoke.

This was the first time I remember reading a book with any depth, and it changed me. It renewed my appreciation of books, giving me a sense of how relevant and powerful they could be. This book in particular taught me a lot about the human condition, mostly about the suffering part of the human condition. Every one of the characters portrayed in *Winesburg, Ohio* is searching outside of themselves for some kind of insight, understanding, emotional fulfillment, or redemption.

Whether it's Elizabeth Willard's loneliness or Elmer Cowley's confusion about how people perceive him, the characters look obsessively to alleviate their suffering through drinking, blaming others, or getting emotionally entangled with others.

I couldn't help but wonder: Why do people suffer so? Why do *I* suffer so? At the time, I didn't really ask those questions out loud, but reading at such a deep level inspired some unconscious spark that I ended up exploring later. It was one of the few times I actually went deeper than a surface reading to find hidden patterns and symbols nodding toward a recurring theme. I was amazed that even at that time—sixty-something years after Anderson wrote the book—we were still talking about the work, discussing the writer's ideas, and reflecting on the human psychology at play in contemporary society.

\*

Enjoy the following exercises. Again, try meditating before writing and see how it goes. May these "reading as becoming" exercises prepare you for the transformative thaw of early spring, helping you spring into action, march into March, and emerge anew in the next chapter with your practice and process.

### Reading Meditation

Read the following passages out loud or silently to yourself:

> Barb, our hospice nurse, has bluish teeth and frizzy black hair styled to look like a hunting cap. The skin around her eyes droops and when you talk to her, she takes too long to respond. She wears loose cotton blouses with patterns of clocks or vines. The woman needs to be startled. In one of the many fantasies I've concocted over the last few weeks here, I own a mess of owls, and they wait, talons clutching the branch in their ornate cage. When Barb comes—when she looks past me to my

mother, past my mother to that voice she listens to when she's not listening to any of us—I will set them free in her face.*
*Robin Romm, The Mercy Papers: A Memoir of Three Weeks (New York: Simon & Schuster, 2009).*

＊

Read the following Q&A from *I Am That* out loud or silently to yourself.

**Q** Where does it [meditation and silence] all lead me?

**A** When the mind is kept away from its preoccupations it becomes quiet. If you do not disturb this quiet and stay in it, you find that it is permeated with a light and love you have never known; and yet you recognize it at once as your own nature. Once you have passed through this experience, you will never be the same man [woman/being] again; the unruly mind may break its peace and obliterate its vision; but it is bound to return, provided the effort is sustained; until the day when all bonds are broken, delusions and attachments end and life becomes supremely concentrated in the present.

**Q** What difference does it make?

**A** The mind is no more. There is only love in action.**
**Nisargadatta Maharaj, I Am That: Talks with Sri Nisargadatta Maharaj (Durham, NC: Acorn Press, 1973).*

＊

**Note: please try the following exercise for *each* of the above passages.**
Find a place to sit comfortably where you can settle your mind and body and won't be interrupted. Gently close your eyes and begin by connecting with the natural rhythm of your breathing in this moment.

Just notice. There's no need to alter your breathing in any way. Just become aware of what's happening with your breathing body. If you feel any obvious tension in your neck or shoulders, go ahead and breathe into those areas and release on the exhale. After having read the above passages, allow the words to simply wash through you. There is nothing to remember or cling to, nothing to figure out or understand. Just let the words be words and your breath be breath, as thought is thought—arising and passing away moment to moment. As you sit here breathing, simply allow yourself to open to whatever is present for you in this moment—whatever emotions, bodily sensations, ideas, urges, fantasies, or plans—just breathe into them and let them go.

After a few minutes, you might notice your mind getting caught up in a train of thought, anticipation, or planning. Simply name it and breathe on. That's your signal to reconnect with the breathing body. Just be here now, halfway between heaven and earth, grounded in the breathing body, celebrating this very moment. Continue breathing and being in this way for five to forty-five minutes as you are able, and finish with the ringing of a bell.

Now go back to each passage above at separate times and reread them, once to yourself and once out loud. Take notes. Note how the first passage is crafted with the written word and the second is transcribed directly from a conversation. One transmits emotion with details and description, whereas the other conveys a spiritual experience with speech. Spend time sitting with this difference and make notes on your own experience of these two kinds of reading/writing.

*Reading/Writing Exercise*

We tend to get stuck in our reading habits—*what* we read and *how* we read. Practice reading on the three levels described earlier in this chapter, starting with a quick skim, then slowing down and rereading. Then give it another go, slowing down to reread, highlight, underline, and rewrite sentences or whole paragraphs. Notice what's different in your experience of the book at each level of reading. Also note how each type of reading affects your writing.

In general, I suggest reading for a minimum of twenty minutes a day in your genre, plus twenty minutes outside of your genre (anything from cereal boxes to magazine articles to Victorian novels), underlining at least ten phrases, sentences, or passages that move you.

Pick a passage from a book you are currently reading. Start with one paragraph, preferably the opening paragraph of the whole book or any one chapter. Ideally, this opening paragraph is filled with sensory detail, interesting twists of phrase, surprising statements, or unique language. From this passage, underline or—even better—rewrite at least five phrases or sentences that surprise, move, or inspire you. Freewrite for ten minutes on what you admire or find unique about this writer's style.

Take this exercise one step further: For a month, make it a weekly practice to rewrite (once by hand, once by typing) an entire page from a favorite author in your genre. What do you notice? Where does your attention lift, and why? Notice your level of excitement or boredom while you read each sentence. What have you learned? What aspect of this writer's style can you incorporate into your own writing?

# Spring

# 3

# March

## {Emergence}

### *Practice and Process*

From our rebirth in January to our expanded state of becoming in February, we press on to further *emergence* in spring. Emerging from one state to the next takes practice and a deep commitment to process. In early spring, life finally bursts through the furtive wreckage of winter, and we march forth on urgent feet, quick-stepping toward the warmth of the sun. Sometimes things warm up just enough to go on a bike ride. I did just that the other day with my friend Jimmi, seeking to escape the clutches of winter by moving my body to open my mind.

This wasn't an ordinary ride. We took our mountain bikes and set off to climb Mount Vision in the Point Reyes National Seashore with the ultimate payoff of getting to descend more than fourteen hundred feet back down to sea level at gloriously high speeds. It was a blustery, crisp day in March with fantastic visibility all the way out to the Farallones, a small set of pointy granite islands thirty miles out to sea from the Golden Gate Bridge. They don't call it Mount Vision for nothing.

We made it to the top and took in the stunning view. Below us lay a dense sun-splintered forest of firs and bishop pines, their alleyways unrolling and dropping into sage-colored mottled grass and scrublands. The shallow hand of Drake's Estero reached into the throat of the peninsula across the curving strip of Limantour Beach, and the chalky cliffs of Drakes Bay stretching out to the north and west at Chimney Rock. The sun shimmered off the curved blue-gray plane of a seemingly endless Pacific.

We each gnawed half an energy bar and readied for the descent. Our trail of choice, Shoemaker's Chute, consists of a steep and twisty route tunneled over by pines and thick ceanothus brush. The trail is approximately the width of an airplane seat in economy. Jimmi went first. I followed, trying to keep up as fast as I could, hoping I wouldn't be decapitated by a low branch or yanked from the bars by some rogue root. Such are the regular hazards of mountain biking in "The Chute." Jimmi banked his first turn at high speed *on his front wheel*, doing what they call a "nose wheelie." I gasped in disbelief as his rear wheel flew up behind him like a loose rudder pulled from the water. All I could do was hold on for dear life with both my wheels on the ground, and I still felt tossed around in one of those dizzying helmet-cam videos in which the landscape whizzes by at an unreasonably dangerous clip. Jimmi banked another turn; this time, his rear wheel tagged high trailside branches. Clearly I was dreaming. This whole scene struck me as unfathomable and absurd—like a hilarious circus act—and the only worthy response was laughter. The exhilaration, the sound of the wind whistling through my helmet, the rapid slap of coffeeberry branches against my shins, the clicks of flimsy limbs against my helmet. And yet, Jimmi sped on, faster and faster. I pedaled right after him, turn after turn, each curve more sketchy than the last, until we finally spit out of the woods into a flat, grassy meadow near the bottom. I threw down my bike and hit the ground with wild convulsive cackles in joyful amazement.

"Jimmi," I said, finally catching my breath, "what the hell was that? Where on earth did you learn to do *that*?"

He popped off his helmet and grinned. "Lots of practice, lots of bravado, and a long and sometimes painful learning curve."

Sounded like writing to me. When I told him that, he nodded. "I guess so," he said. "And probably both require your serious undivided attention. Riding like this does, that's for sure."

Jimmi calls it land-based flying. When I head down the open space of a blank page and give myself completely to my writing, it feels like flying.

Riding is not unlike writing: weaving through space; threading a high-speed path through the woods of thought; leaving an invisible script upon the land, an ode to movement and grace, speed and balance, at one with the body, bike, landscape, sun, and air—minus space, minus time.

Jimmi has been on a bike virtually nonstop since he was four. At eleven, he jumped eight garbage cans on his neighbor Colleen Baldwin's Schwinn Step-Through Stingray and made it. As a young adult, he raced motocross semiprofessionally, and although he doesn't compete anymore (he's fifty-four now) he's one of the most highly skilled cyclists around. He thoroughly enjoys riding, making the experience edgy and fun for himself and an occasional fortunate friend. In other words, Jimmi cares a lot about biking; he's not a dabbler—cycling is Jimmi's practice. He emphasized how much practice it takes to emerge from cautious fire-road lollygagger to exhilarated land-flyer, running nose wheelies down technical singletrack. I thought of the occasional scribbler versus the attentive and consistent journalist, novelist, memoirist, or poet.

It takes a lot to write, edit, and complete a book. In addition to practice, there's balance, strength, and research—a thrilling blend akin to riding a mountain bike high-speed through tight trees and chunky rock gardens. For both, the rewards are innumerable—the exhilaration of practice, the experience of emerging to a new level of proficiency, deep satisfaction, and confidence; and—often when getting pulled along into the speedy emotional current of an inspiring writing session—a whole lot of laughter.

*

There's a term thrown around in the world of writing that I've never fully understood: *emerging writer*. To emerge as a writer, or anything else for that matter, you must emerge from one thing into an entirely different something else—that is, you must move from one state of being or existence to another. As a writer, that only happens through practice.

I like to define *writer* as someone who writes, not someone who is published for their writing per se. Let me qualify that a little: a writer is someone who writes regularly and consistently, someone who engages in the process. If you give yourself to that process, if you do the work, if you write regularly and consistently, then you are not *emerging* as a writer—you are already engaged, you are already a practicing writer. What it takes to go from *emerging* to *emerged* is a shift of perception followed by consistent action. It's like being a couch potato, becoming a couch surfer, and eventually transforming into a couch creator. You're dealing with couches in one way or the other the whole time; it's just that you've swapped the bowl of potato chips for a laptop or your favorite notebook and pen. Sometimes it really is that simple. You go from the idea of writing (one potato, two potato, crunch, crunch)—that is, fantasizing about writing "one of these days"—to actually signing up for that fiction class, poetry workshop, or writing retreat. You take in the inspiration, knowledge, and motivation you get from that and then, finally, sit your butt down in the chair (or upright on the couch, chips back in the sealed bag and locked in the cabinet) every day for the next year (or ten) and write the damn thing. For the record, I write on my couch every day, without chips. But heck, as long as you're writing consistently and you're capable of multitasking, crunch away!

Emergence means sticking with the practice long enough until you've experienced a sense of improvement, growth, and even transformation. Sometimes this takes minutes, sometimes years. Emergence is also about taking time to connect with your deeper self, touching into your creative desires and true intentions, and exploring the hidden layers of yourself that call out to be expressed. The timing for when we emerge, or when the writing emerges from within us, is a highly personal one and ultimately a decision that we shouldn't put off until some nebulous future moment—not if we sincerely want to write. In other words, stop thinking and start writing.

I thought about writing for years and wrote nothing. Then I wrote in fits and starts. Then I wrote obscure (mostly) experimental poetry for fifteen years or so, which was fun and interesting and I learned a lot about craft in the process (heck, I even finished countless writing projects and published several small books along the way). And yet I was still writing only on occasion, still emerging. If I'm honest with myself, I was writing around my vulnerabilities, avoiding the deeper emotions, the truer story lurking within—until I couldn't take it anymore. I had become so haunted by childhood scenes and memories—some difficult yet compelling images—that begged to be written down. Something bigger was gnawing at me, yearning to emerge. Around this time my friends and neighbors recommended several memoirs that inspired me to give it a shot. Reading books like *Running with Scissors*, *Tender at the Bone*, and *Wild* was like having having the authors themselves shouting words of insight, encouragement, and permission. The next thing I knew, I was writing a memoir.

Emergence is about showing up, about materialization—going from the nonphysical to the physical—from the darkness and mystery of incubation to the light of manifestation. To move from scattered ideas, broken dreams, and those frustratingly inconsistent false starts to solid discipline and completion, we need to first shift our thinking and then adjust our physical behavior—literally *how* we interact with the couch (or wherever it is we can finally get some writing done).

If you truly want to write—if you feel genuinely curious about this writing business and your potential to take part in it—you have to make time to do it, and that means you need to set some kind of schedule. I recently surveyed thousands of writers and would-be writers who are on my mailing list, and the number-one thing they reported struggling with the most was time. Remember, time is not something that you have or don't have—time is something you create. What are your priorities? What could you shift or tweak in your daily life to create some space for your writing? You have to make time to write if you are sincere in your desire to manifest your writing dreams. And if you are just too darn busy with work, kids, and life, then make your writing a kind of squeezing-in practice: squeeze it in on your lunch break, in the car while waiting to pick up the kids, in the morning, with your favorite flavor of caffeine coursing through your veins, by waking up fifteen minutes earlier than usual. If it's important, you'll find the time. I know writers who rent motel rooms for occasional weekends of concentrated binge writing, and one who records voice memos (that eventually grow into novels) while she's stopped in traffic during her daily commute.

You've heard it over and over again, that annoying little adage about writing being a practice. The thing that often gets left out of the conversation around practice is how unappetizing the initial idea of practice actually is. You can hear the nagging parent or teacher in the back of your head, "Okay, Mary, it's time to practice your scales," when you'd rather be hanging out with your friends playing freeze tag or rearranging your sock drawer. *Practice*. That word voiced in our heads sometimes echoes ominously like scolding thunder; it seems to come with built-in resistance. Who wants to *practice*? It can sound so arduous and even unappealing, like a chore that needs to be completed. But the key aspect of practice that we often forget is the discovery and enchantment we get along the way. After giving myself to the practice of writing for more than twenty years, I know the more I practice, the more I learn not only about the art itself but also about my own quietly evolving heart and mind. I learn more about consciousness itself. It's fascinating, really. It's not so much that I, Albert, am so fascinating—it's that we as humans are fascinating. You are inherently interesting beyond compare, and you will become even more so when you take the time to delve deep and write forth your inner truth.

> **TRY THIS**  Schedule times for your writing practice. Calendar it now (or at least sometime today) like you would an appointment with your dentist, doctor, or tax accountant. Alert your loved ones, your friends, your neighbors. What—you don't have time to write for fifteen minutes, five days a week? Of course you do. Go to bed fifteen minutes later, get up fifteen minutes earlier. Don't think too much about it. Find your nook, set your timer (or not), and write for fifteen minutes (or longer if you can squeeze it in)—just go. Work with an existing project or begin with a new random prompt just to get yourself going and in the habit. Commit. Make it a habit, a ritual.

**AND THIS**   Take fifteen minutes during your lunch break at work to practice walking meditation. Breathe. Lift foot, place foot. Step. Breathe. Lift foot, place foot. Step. Breathe. Walk. Repeat. Keep your gaze soft and spacious, positioned between the ground and your eyes. Connect with the movements of your body. Breathe into the experience of its motions. Don't make a scene of it by walking like a zombie across your cafeteria, but find an uncrowded area nearby or walk around the block, slowly and mindfully. Notice the difference between this pace and the way you normally walk. Breathe in deeply, exhale. Enjoy the miracle of simply walking.

When I first contemplated writing a memoir, my first thought was, "No way! I have a terrible memory!" I marveled at my favorite memoirists—Augusten Burroughs, Mary Karr, Nick Flynn, Ruth Reichl, Cheryl Strayed, and Elizabeth Gilbert, to name a few—and wondered how in the hell they remembered all those grisly brilliant details from their childhoods. Seriously, how could they remember the color of the hand towels in their parents' bathroom? Or what the babysitter wore when she offered them a joint? But they didn't. I mean, they remembered something but not the things *exactly as written*. That's called poetic license, and you earn that license when you commit fully to the practice and process of writing, and it works no matter whether you write memoirs, fiction, short stories, scripts, plays, personal essays, or poetry. As Ron Padgett writes in his poem "Poetic License":

> This license certifies
> That Ron Padgett may tell whatever lies
> His heart desires
> Until it expires

Writing memoir is an act of emergence by the mere fact that the process requires you to reflect on your being in the world and how you as a person or character have evolved over time—what you emerged from and then into. Your poetic license is your license to remember, and in effect reconstruct your memory around the most significant situations of your life. Needless to say, it's an emotionally courageous and often taxing process that requires patience, perseverance, and flexibility. Your poetic license enables you to free yourself from your old story and emerge into a new narrative of a transformed person who is no longer held hostage by the terrors and restrictions of the past.

We like to think of memoir as fact; it's "nonfiction," after all. The writer has faithfully reported on what happened in their life, right? Kind of. Sometimes a memoir writer does have exceptional memories. Sometimes the author kept a journal, sometimes they interviewed a family member. But most likely what happened is this: they sat down and wrote into those (often difficult) memories to the best of their conjuring abilities, and reported back as if to say "this is how I remember it" or "it felt something like this." Memoir as a literary genre is considered creative nonfiction—emphasis on the word *creative*—in which we get to exercise our poetic license (within reason—more on the morality and boundaries of poetic license in chapter 5). These writers are not writing their memoirs as they might an autobiography: *First, I was born, and then this particular thing happened, and then this specific other thing happened, etc.* And even there, memory is a slippery eel. When we call up a memory and turn it around in our head and then write it down, subsequent memories naturally surface; that's the nature of memory and language. The more you engage it, the more it gives back and propagates. Writing memoir, or any genre for that matter, is an act of emergence, an act of discovery, if only for the fact that all writing is autobiographical in some sense, if even vaguely. Every moment, every writing session, can reveal a new layer of insight, new memories, or a new angle on an ancient theme. This is why, as a meetup writing group in San Francisco advises, we must simply remain curious, stop thinking about it, and at a certain point just "shut up and write."

## WRITING OUR WAY TO ENCHANTMENT

When we finally surrender and commit to a daily writing practice and simply freewrite our way into a process, writing our way through the resistances and into the stream of our own consciousness, we naturally become more curious, more surprised. We start to see the wild diversity of ideas brewing within us, our creative potential shining through. We can't help but become more enchanted with ourselves and the mad diversity of the world. We begin to burrow down into the vast depth of our own heart and mind where compassion, insight, and understanding can blossom, and where the barriers between self and other disappear.

*

The famous American street photographer Garry Winogrand took thousands of photographs every week. For every one hundred rolls of film he shot, Winogrand might get a dozen interesting pictures. He was out there on the street every day shooting from the hip. He drove around the country visiting food stalls at country markets, busy city streets, rodeos, carnivals, and desolate suburban culs-de-sac (where he might have photographed my friend Jimmi jumping garbage cans). He visited aquariums, airports, supermarkets, vacant lots, and crowded beaches, all the while taking pictures, capturing the wild instants of his seeing. This was his version of being present—"enlightenment in daily life endlessly," as Zen master Dogen puts it. Winogrand was seeking not only a flash or two of America and its people but also to understand what stirred deeply in his own heart and mind. A lot of the time he didn't even bring the camera up to his eye.

The equivalent for us writers is freewriting: seeing (writing) before the self-critical invasion of thinking. This means observing and writing every day, engaging the writing process to know how and what you think. This is your practice and process. Through that process you start to experience a more raw, immediate, and unadulterated interaction with the senses. After a while, you find yourself able to capture an unexpected, unseen, mysterious emotionality, and an unfiltered beauty *emerges* in your writing as it did for Winogrand in his pictures—mostly because he kept showing up with camera in hand. Your job is to show up simply like this—pen in hand—and write forth the raw immediacy of your experience with courageous authenticity. You never know what's going to happen, what you're going to create in any given moment. The artist needs to remain open and alert, practicing *all* the time. Several of Winogrand's most compelling photographs were shot from the hip, his version of freewriting. Several of my favorite sections of this book, as well as scenes in my new novel, *Brooklyn, Wyoming*, were originally written as freewrites—urgent, immediate, and alive, without overthinking, doubting, making snap judgments, or self-censoring. Winogrand knew that tapping into the universe of his mind while engaging the wacky and unpredictable world was the recipe for making great art. He stepped into an expansive field of light, an electric and kinetic space crackling with the vitality of daily life moment to moment. As long as he was there with his camera he could capture some of its magic and share it with the world. And he did—over and over again.

His medium was light. Ours is the written word. The more you engage and play with words through writing—turning them over in your heart and mind, flipping through moods and feelings, moments and days—the more likely insight, beauty, and inspiration will emerge from within you.

## THE ART OF EMERGENCE

Here's how to emerge from one state to the next through practice:

*Practice doesn't make perfect, practice makes process, and with consistent attention, proficiency, and eventually, with further devotion, mastery.* I don't know why that's in italics, except for emphasis. Even though it's already written down, write those words again by hand in your notebook. Or type it up in bold script and put it along the top rim of your computer monitor, bulletin board, or writing altar. What? You don't have a writing altar? You should! (More on that later.)

Many of us struggle with maintaining a practice and staying consistent in order to develop a process. The constant striving for an imagined sense of perfection is one of the things that can keep us off the page. If perfection is your jam, say this out loud, in all caps for emphasis. THERE IS NO SUCH THING AS PERFECTION. Recite it often! Perfection is an idealized fantasy-state conjured up by I don't know who, but it simply doesn't exist. Now, having said that, I will say that hard work, study, practice, rewriting, professional editing, and even more rewriting *are* essential. It's so easy to delude ourselves and think we've taken our writing to the limit, when we haven't really taken it as far as we could. So we either put it aside and move on to another project, or push on a little bit further until we think we can't take it anymore. And maybe at some point we reach consensus with a majority of outside readers, who tell us it's time to take another step, to go ahead and publish the damn thing. This process takes extreme patience and honesty with ourselves coupled with a willingness to push beyond what we thought we could do.

For this reason, meditation can be incredibly helpful to writers. It challenges us constantly to move beyond our perceived limitations and capacities. We talk ourselves out of things all the time. You'd be amazed at how many people claim they could never sit still for twenty minutes in silence, as if they would explode or go instantly crazy. Nonsense. Anyone can do it. All you have to do is start with two or three minutes and work up to longer periods. It's the same with writing. People tell themselves they could never write a full-length novel, but when they actually sit down to write and knock out several hundred words or a couple of pages in all of five minutes, they realize they still have plenty more to say.

I regularly meet people who have a fairly broad definition of meditation. They consider anything that requires focus and some level of slowing down to be meditation—gardening, doing the dishes, sewing, trail running, fishing, and so on. Just so we're clear, what I'm calling meditation here is something more than activities that help soothe and ground us. Such activities are helpful and fun, but to me they don't quite qualify as *meditation*. Real meditation is not something that you can learn from a blog post, download on iTunes, or even master from a great book, though all these resources may be wonderful *introductions* to meditation. Meditation is more than concentration or patterned focus—it's a complete turning inward and letting go. It starts with following your internal experience by using the breath as your guide, and eventually enables you to touch true emptiness, making contact with Source itself, going far beyond mere words and explanations. Ultimately, we have to find out for ourselves, in our own direct experience, what is true. Meditation allows us to do that. So no matter your level of experience with meditation, I invite you to go deep within and find out for yourself.

*

There was a guy I knew from my meditation community. He knew all the teachers at Spirit Rock and had studied with a number of famous spiritual guides and gurus. One night we were sitting in his car in the rain, waiting to pick up his girlfriend at the airport, when I asked him how his meditation practice was going. He answered, "Oh, I stopped meditating months ago."

"Seriously? I thought you'd been practicing for thirty years!"

"Yeah, but I wasn't getting anywhere."

I just stared at him in shock, my jaw slack with disbelief. I think I even stuttered.

He continued, "I wasn't progressing, so I just stopped. Formal sitting practice, that is. But, you know, I still consider making art a kind of meditation."

I sort of couldn't believe it. "No *progress*? It hasn't gotten you anywhere? But that's the f-ing point!" I protested (well, in my head). There is nothing to gain, nowhere to go, nothing to change. This is the big joke of meditation and the hardest thing for us in our Western culture with minds habituated to consumerism and accumulation to get: we're already awake. I know it might be hard to believe, but to surrender to practice and process *is* the path to awakening. There's nothing more to do or *get*. And the more we can enjoy the practice and process, the more likely we are to emerge as an awakened being!

*

Start by practicing your writing openly, spontaneously, and consistently. Do it whenever you can, and soon a methodical process will emerge, giving birth to your voice and style like some bent and broken petal-torn clover rising up through the hardpan of a dusty vacant lot. Eventually that clover will straighten, its petals will heal, color will flush through, and it will beam bright! The timing is uncertain and ultimately not up to you. Patience and perseverance are your friends, so snuggle up close. Your job is to show up, shut up, and write.

Below you'll find a general outline of the rough and continually evolving process I've developed over years of writing. This process has helped me emerge from an erratic, inconsistent, and procrastinating scribbler to a devoted writer and widely published author. Note: this process looks a little different depending on what genre I'm writing in—my practice for writing poetry doesn't look like my practice for writing a novel. There is no singular correct writing process; it's a unique experience that should develop organically over time, based on your life situation and learning pace. Think of the following example as just that: one example among millions. Feel free to tweak it and make it your own.

> **Step 1    Starting out and stepping in—research and reading.**
> Whenever I begin a new writing project, I start by reading
> heavily in my project's particular genre. I read carefully and
> diversely. I conduct a little research to flare up the sparks of
> interest. I reread and read some more. I underline and take
> notes. I look for resonant models that inspire me toward my
> own ideas.

> **Step 2    Putting pen to paper/fingers to keys.** I begin with
> prospective titles and initial concepts and write into them
> every day, sometimes for an hour, sometimes for five or six.
> For a novel, memoir, or some form of nonfiction, I start with
> initial ideas and images, perhaps an anecdote that resonates
> in my mind. I write it all down: notes, freewrites, character
> sketches, descriptive scenes, my cast of characters (who wants

to be in this book and why? what purpose will they serve?), chapter headings, and other points that seem important. Honestly, I'm a bit manic and spontaneous at this point—I feel compelled to put down fast and furiously whatever's there, with a kind of blind excitement and urgency, before I can think myself into doubt and second guesses. This goes on for between three and six months, depending on the project and its length, until I have accumulated something in the range of fifty thousand to one hundred thousand words. I do not worry about spelling and punctuation, grammar and usage. I do not fret over whether I or anyone else likes it or will even see it. It's my extremely rough (in technical terms, "shitty") first draft, but I learn to love it as a foundation, warts and all. I press on.

**Step 3   Rereading, re-visioning, rearranging.** I then spend a few weeks rereading the material and highlighting the strongest pages, the ones that seem bright and alive for me, those that offer energy or something of interest. At this point, I might assemble pieces into sections or chapters.

**Step 4   Editing in earnest.** Let the editing begin, for real. I remove dead or redundant sections, moving them to my "compost" folder in the event I might want to revisit them at a later date. I then add details to scenes, write into my characters, tinker with the dialogue, flush out characters' motives and roles, and write into the descriptions with more specificity.

**Step 5   Journeying through the great dark editing forest.** The editing continues. I begin with large passages, then focus on paragraphs, looking to delete, trim down, and add detail. I might hack twenty thousand words and write an entirely new twenty thousand at this point, now that I am fully immersed in the process and new ideas are flowing through me on a weekly basis. I'm beginning to home in on what I think the project is about, gathering more clarity about its essence and what I want to achieve.

**Step 6   Getting professional help.** At this point (after the third draft or so), I have an editor help me with the big picture, and we go through a developmental edit, which focuses on the elements of structure and form—the chapters, sections, general flow of the narrative or main ideas, and primary themes. We identify gaps in the organization and clarify areas that need more attention.

**Step 7   Digesting, discerning, and integrating.** After digesting and integrating the feedback from the developmental edit, I dive into a fourth draft, honing paragraphs and sentences, adding stronger verbs, hyper-detailing my images, sharpening my metaphors and similes, deleting flat sentences, and adding new ones along with entirely new paragraphs and even sections. This process goes on for weeks or months, honing and refining, adding and deleting. Tinkering, as it were. After some time—a year, maybe two—the writing starts to feel solid.

**Step 8   Calling in your trusted readers.** At this point, I bring in more readers—three or more trusted friends and colleagues with varying tastes—to see what they think. After asking for constructive feedback and being specific about what I'm looking for, I generally take things with a grain of salt. Mostly I ask them to let me know where the work feels a little stuck, a little off, and what specific sections or chapters need help. I also ask them to tell me what's working, what they like. I pay attention to repeated responses from my readers—that is, areas where their feedback overlaps. If three of them mention how one particular scene falls flat or seems extraneous, I probably need to work on that scene. If one of my readers loves a particular passage, one thinks it's just okay, and the third can't stand it, then I reread it out loud to myself and reexamine how it works or doesn't work. I try to be careful with outside opinions—some are definitely more valuable than others. As a general rule, I never let them sway the primary intent of my work. What I'm looking for is insight and consensus; if I can't find that from friends and colleagues, I hire a professional editor.

**Step 9   Revisiting professional feedback.** Whether self-publishing or using an agent and going with a major publishing house, I find it absolutely necessary to work with a professional editor. Note that this step only comes after I go through a developmental edit and get feedback from readers that I trust.

**Step 10   Giving it a rest, letting it cure, and pressing on.** While the editor is doing his or her job, I let the manuscript sit for a few days, weeks, or even months. I try to do something else—go on vacation, learn to play the ukulele, start a garden. This ensures that I come back to the manuscript with a fresh perspective. When I hear back from the editor, I thoroughly digest the suggested edits, ask them any questions I might have, and then block out some serious time over the next few months to polish, polish, polish. I tinker and play, get down to the level of individual words, and try to construct the most beautiful and detailed sentences I can. I delete, rewrite, freewrite, sculpt, play, and polish again until it all feels *right*. I want my ideas to feel clear and well presented; I want everything to flow and dance in meaningful patterns. At this stage, I regularly feel bursts of insight and moments of inspiration—I even feel pride at my commitment to the process and the work itself. At the end of the day, the writing process is a combination of intuition, practice, feedback integration, perseverance, and—most importantly—patience.

**Step 11   Celebrating.** At this point, I celebrate. I make dinner for my reader friends or have them make dinner for me. Anything, really, to celebrate this milestone, this recognition of the heroic journey I've just completed. Then I take another break and send the manuscript off to my agent or publisher. Eventually, the writing finds its way out into the world, finally connecting with its readers.

*

I hope this outline gives you a sense of practice and process in action. Now it's your turn to burst into the heart of spring with a revolutionary introduction (or reintroduction) to poetry—the ground of all great writing. The following emergence exercises will help launch you into the next chapter and prepare you for a deeper understanding of poetry and its potential to transform your writing and your life!

### → *Emergence Meditation Exercise*

Let's start again by finding a comfortable place to sit. Relax, but sit upright so that your breath can flow easily throughout your body. Gently close your eyes and simply become aware of your breathing body. What's it like to be embodied in this moment? You have nothing to do right now, nothing to figure out or fix, nothing to learn or understand, nothing to accomplish or even control. Just sit here breathing, letting thoughts be thoughts, sensations be sensations, allowing everything to be as it is. You are emerging from a thinking, discerning, and controlling mind to an open and free mind of allowance and curiosity. Let things arise and pass away as is their nature.

Now bring your awareness or attention to any place in your body that may be experiencing sensation in this moment. A stirring in your belly, an ache in your neck, a cramp in your leg. Breathe into this spot in your body, noticing the emergence of its energy. It may be subtle or fairly dramatic. Simply notice its emergence, stay present with it all the way through to its recession and disappearance. Notice any thoughts or feelings about this sensation, and how that expands or contracts the physical feelings. Be awake to the emergence of sensation within you and watch it disappear, as is its natural ebb and flow. Just observe and notice. There is nothing to fix or change right now. If you experience pain, emotional or otherwise, breathe into the experience with as much compassion and patience as you can muster. Breathe in, breathe out, letting go one breath at a time. Open your eyes to conclude the meditation.

—◆—

### Emergence Freewriting Exercise

For the next week, I want you to take a camera around with you every day, even if it's just the camera on your smartphone. Wander around looking, noticing, staying awake to your environment. In this exercise, I invite you to participate more deeply in your sensory experience in order to *emerge* from passive glancer to immersed, specifically attuned, emotionally moved, and engaged viewer. Take pictures of what interests you—colors, movements, contrasts, beautiful objects or people, the shock and weirdness of street scenes. Don't think too much about it—just take pictures of whatever catches your eye. Hold the camera in different positions (at your hip, down by your feet, etc.), playing with the perspective, remaining quick and spontaneous. Have fun and don't overthink it. Remember, you can delete all of these photos at the end of the week. Take at least twenty pictures a day, minimum. At the end of the week, scroll through and pick three favorites from each day. I'm not asking you to pick the "best" photos per se; instead, pick the ones you find funny, colorful, or surprising. From those twenty-one photos (seven days, three photos each), choose your three favorites.

Here's the writing assignment: freewrite for at least twenty minutes on each picture, dedicating a different writing session for each (for example, one photograph per day). Start by describing in as much detail as you can what's in the picture—the colors, shapes, scene, people, landscape, and so on. Then write about what's beyond or outside the frame: What's the story of this picture? How did this scene come to be? Who are these people and objects? What's their history? Let your imagination run wild. If the ideas still flow after twenty minutes, keep going for as long as you want, or until the energy subsides. Have fun and enjoy watching your amazing images, ideas, and insights emerge!

# 4

# April

## {Blossoming}

*Poetry: The Language of Possibility*

The great American poet Carl Sandburg writes, "Poetry is an echo asking a shadow to dance." That definition doesn't bring us any closer to an understanding of what poetry is, nor does it make much sense in the traditional, logical meaning of the word *sense*. But is it sensory? Does it spark your imagination? Does it open your heart and mind, your bodily awareness? Does it trigger a hunger for deeper exploration? As intellectual, ego-driven humans we want to figure it out—we want to know what things *mean*. What could Sandburg's definition possibly mean? Maybe that's the wrong question. Maybe it doesn't *mean* anything—and that's precisely the point! We can't do anything with it, we can't buy or sell it, or even figure it out—it's simply strange and beautiful. It incites a kind of urgent curiosity and wonder, sparks the miracle of the imagination in this moment, which then becomes a moment of mystery and possibility. This is the power of poetry to incite awe and wonder, to inspire great writing.

Now, what if we replaced the word *poetry* in Sandburg's definition with the word *I*? As in "*I* am an echo asking a shadow to dance." Doing so, we become an agent of energy, an object of curiosity and wonder, a generator of imagination and possibility. This is the role of poetry and all writing—to serve as the conduit for an evolutionary and inspirational consciousness. This is writing as a path to awakening.

How do we articulate the miraculous in speech or writing? In "East Coker," in his Four Quartets, T.S. Eliot describes poetry as "a raid on the inarticulate." That is to say, poetry is an incursion into the realm of the confoundingly unsayable. Now you, dear reader, are a living, breathing miracle—a divine expression of the inarticulate. In a million years we could never write forth the full, brilliant, unsayable complexity of who you truly are. Whether you see yourself this way or not, it's the truth. Apparently we have six trillion biochemical interactions occurring within our bodies per second. (I feel sorry for the sucker who had to count them all.) How's that for being a miraculous organism? Given such a vast and incalculable self, how do we go about describing it?

The word *poem* comes from the Greek word *poiein*, which means "to make, to do, to create." The poet *is* a creator. In the previous chapter, I stated that poetry is the ground for all great writing, partly because I started as a poet myself, and partly because—through years of reading, writing, and discussions with other writers—I have found that all great writing has its origins in the musicality, rhythm, images, and rich metaphoric language of poetry. Going forward, we could use the word *poet* broadly to mean "an enlightened (creative) human citizen," and that means all of us: poet-mechanics, poet-teachers, poet-entrepreneurs, poet-doctors, poet-firefighters, poet-moms, poet–street sweepers, and so on. Not that I want you all to become poets literally. Rather, I want to encourage you to not only write poetically, but also to live your life poetically—that is to say, creatively, with an inevitable cosmic luminosity; with presence, grace, and beauty woven in.

✻

Around the time I attended my first meditation retreat, I started working with kids through the California Poets in the Schools program. Kids are natural creative geniuses, and when you meet them directly with love, curiosity, and genuine interest in *their* take on the world, poetry full of wisdom and insight spills forth from them. I soon realized that working with kids was the most important work I could do in the world. If people feel inspired to remember who they really are (as infinite creative geniuses), we can change the world. If people have a safe, open place to express their authentic emotional experiences, we can change everything!

> Turquoise laughter
> An eagle in the sky
> A butterfly whispering
> In a dragonfly's ear,
> The angels peering in
> The corner window
> Just like a poet weaving
> her story
> on a loom of sawdust

That's from Caroline Calhoun, who was nine years old at the time. She called the poem "Secrets." What magic, what sensibility, what insight and wonder! This is writing on the path to awakening, an expression of imagination that radiates out, inspiring the hearts and minds of other students, teachers, parents, and the larger community. I read this poem in front of a meeting of the Board of Supervisors for my county, when I was sworn in as poet laureate, and the people who heard it were amazed by these words of joy and imaginative delight.

Whether you are writing a poem, a novel, an essay, a play, or a memoir, I want to encourage you to express your heart's desire with full abandon. Whether you're dancing a dance, building a building, running a company, chauffeuring a kid to soccer practice, or leading a country, I want to inspire you to do it with your unique aesthetic sensibility and a reverence for life. Can you slow down enough to weave in such poetic awareness? In the midst of this massive, glorious, and bewildering maelstrom of technology and convenience, can you write forth your divine self along this mysterious path to awakening?

Yes! The answer is yes, you can. And I beg you to do so. Don't lose sight of who you *really* are—a creator and integrator of a poetic evolutionary consciousness. Your life, your community, your world depends on it. We need you to weave *your* story on a loom of sawdust!

*

A poetic interlude, brought to you by E.E. Cummings:

Paris;this April sunset completely
utters

Paris;this April sunset completely utters
utters serenely silently a cathedral

before whose upward lean magnificent face
the streets turn young with rain,

spiral acres of bloated rose
coiled within cobalt miles of sky
yield to and heed
the mauve
   of twilight(who slenderly descends,
daintily carrying in her eyes the dangerous first stars)
people move love hurry in a gently

arriving gloom and
see!(the new moon
fills abruptly with sudden silver
these torn pockets of lame and begging colour)while
there and here the lithe indolent prostitute
Night,argues

with certain houses

One could write a thousand pages on this poem and all its brilliant nooks and crannies of beauty, symbolism, and truth, but that's not why I include it here. This poem becomes a perfect example of the impossibility of defining or even talking about poetry, and yet we seem to have a need to articulate some sense of how to work with it as a powerful influencer, teacher, and progenitor, not only of language but also of being itself. As a friend recently reminded me, *we are meaning-making machines*. And yet, as the singer-songwriter Iris DeMent writes, "I think I'll just let the mystery be."

**TRY THIS**   Do you have some favorite poems? Poems that you were told to memorize in school? Poems that your parents or grandparents read to you? Poems you heard at weddings or funerals? Explore a little bit. Unearth what comes up and make a list. Read these poems again and find new ones before your next writing or meditation session.

Is poetry something new to your experience? Start by going to the library and paging through poetry anthologies. Browse through poems on poets.org until you find something that rings true for you. What draws your attention, surprises you, stirs your heart and mind? Find individual books by poets that speak to you and read their work as you are inclined.

Defining poetry is like trying to drink in the wind, like writing on water, or like talking to god. How do you define *god, truth, emptiness,* or even *awakening*? The short answer is you don't. Instead, you write around it, pointing in its general direction. It's a beautifully futile practice of yearning toward becoming and arriving at where you already are. It's a circumambulation of the heart and mind—a reverse, counterintuitive, and contradictory returning. Defining poetry is an interestingly absurd attempt at talking about that which can't be spoken, that which can't be written—and yet speak and write we do. Poetry is the language of possibility. It's an act of emergence; it's the essence of creation, impulse, and imagination erupting from the void—the space between words that makes or breaks its enactment. Music is made by the pauses between the notes. In poetry, silence is the only appropriate response.

Let me expand on that: I want to use the word *blossoming* to take us forward. After all, it is April (and even if it isn't April as you read this, let your mind take you there), and things blossom in April, and yet they also die. Poetry concerns itself with these things—the cycles of living and dying, the great bloomings and witherings away. Trying to write through and into the profound mystery of things, continuously "raiding the inarticulate"—why bother? One answer might be found in the need to keep the conversation going, to keep pointing. And just because you can't define something through words doesn't mean you shouldn't keep yearning for its possibilities to burn through you. As a writer, keep touching into this mystery; keep inviting your reader again and again to drop the book, turn inward, and bathe in the silences. Lean into that "sudden silver" of a sunset evening in Paris, in April, in love with the moment. Ask your readers to fall back into the enigmatic mirror of the self "coiled within cobalt miles of sky" and breathe into that which makes breath possible. Give your readers the opportunity to see and feel for themselves what is true through language and what is true within themselves.

The call is to focus on the unfocusable. Write your way through blue air, tightrope walk across a skinny, blond horizon, hopscotch atop mottled clouds. Scrawl bodily about through plum-dark water until you go blank from the bubbly disappearances. Take time to gather strands of sunlight by the hand, as you might a bouquet of laughing daffodils, letting everything you touch shine forth through your blazing fingertips. Poetry is your guide; poetry will take you there. Language is your material as clay is to potters, paint to painters, body and space to dancers, sound and silence to musicians. So, get sculpting, get painting, get dancing and singing.

Begin by getting your hands on some basic tools, such as a good dictionary. Dive in and swim around. If you can afford it, go with the *Oxford English Dictionary*; if not, I recommend *Merriam-Webster's Unabridged*. Check out the *Princeton Encyclopedia of Poetry and Poetics*. Flip through it, fondle it, lay your weary head upon it (for proper absorption), and—finally—read it. And books, lots of them, from all genres, but especially books of poetry. My friend Cheryl Strayed advises a young writer in one of her "Dear Sugar" columns to "write like a motherfucker." Absolutely. And so to that I would simply add: read poetry like a motherfucker. What one weighty luxury did Cheryl not burn but end up carrying for the duration of her now famous backpacking trip along the Pacific Crest Trail? A copy of *The Dream of a Common Language* by the late poet Adrienne Rich. This is a great example of the power of poetry to soothe and guide, nourish and even heal—that is, read poetry with full abandon. It doesn't matter what your preferred genre is: personal essay, memoir, fiction, nonfiction, scripts for TV or the stage, even poetry itself. Read all things poetic. What does that mean? How will you know that it's *poetic*? Here's a brief guide:

1. **Muse-i-cality.** You will hear music and rhythm in the language. You will encounter repetition, alliteration, rhyme, assonance, and reasonlessness. You will come across slant rhyme, off rhyme, royal rhyme, counterpoint rhyme, and rhyme drenched in limes (sorry). You will also hear onomatopoeic creatures slushing, squawking, crunching, shneeping, and thwapping.

2. **Physicality.** You will read lines instead of complete sentences. Okay? /Okay/could be its own line. Lines/are broken-up sentences/using these slashes/when denoting/line breaks/ in a sentence/about lines. And you will meet stanzas, those postcoital paragraphs—blissed out, dreamy, and relaxed, feeling that anything is possible. Think of stanzas as paragraphs with the hiccups, on diet pills, with tangential distractible attitude—good ol' erratic and unpredictable arrangements of lines.

3. **Spaciousness.** You will see that poets use space on the page for words to move and organize themselves in unique and unexpected ways (often called concrete poetry, visual poetry, or shaped poetry). The words will appear as strands raining down the page, or as puffs of clouds, or as birds on the horizon (when they are actually just lost letters looking for their flock).

4. **Form into formlessness.** You will find forms: sonnets (fourteen lines); ballades (three stanzas of five, seven, eight, or ten lines);

haiku (a short Japanese form that records the essence of a moment involving nature, juxtaposition, and impermanence); sestinas (six unrhymed stanzas in a rolling pattern in which the ending words of the first stanza's lines recur at the ends of all the other stanzas' lines, concluding with a tercet—a three-lined stanza). And that's just the beginning. Try one out for yourself without looking at the definition. The beautiful thing with poetry is you can't go wrong.

5. **Allegoric-mytho-symbology.** You will ponder personifications, metaphors, and similes. Nonhuman objects will become animate: the sun will frown, the rain will smile, rage will strut down the hallway wearing a red cape and crimson boots, love will fly away on fuchsia wings. And relationships will be expressed in words linking unlike things. The sun might appear as a polished copper penny. A bird might transform into a blue arrow, a pond at dusk looks like a circle of black cloth (Mary Oliver), a voice builds itself into a pillar of ashes (Federico García Lorca), a tongue shows up in a mouth like a wet sneaker (from a story I read in the *New Yorker*), a thought slips your mind like a blob of ketchup sliding from a wet plate (a fourth-grade student you'll read about in the next chapter).

6. **Radiating imagistics.** You will encounter miraculous images—dense clusters of sensory words. You might enter an empty room with a single green high-heeled shoe wrapped in a red bow turned over in the corner. Or see a child wearing a silver birthday hat standing in a coffin. Or a pot of boiled white potatoes knocked to the floor, with a ribbon of blood trickling toward it (Anton Chekhov). Or a black vulture coiling its way to the heavens, its yard-wide wings catching the last of the setting sun.

*

You will find all this and more. Poetry is the song of god, the gateway for the divine inspiring you to wake up to your own inherent, wondrous creativity. Poetry realigns us with that original enchantment we felt with the world when we were kids. It is the vehicle to express that wonder—the yearning to return to inspiration and awe. As the legendary Lawrence Ferlinghetti puts it in his poem "I Am Waiting":

> . . . and I am waiting
> for forests and animals
> to reclaim the earth as theirs
> and I am waiting
> for a way to be devised
> to destroy all nationalisms
> without killing anybody
> and I am waiting
> for linnets and planets to fall like rain
> and I am waiting for lovers and weepers
> to lie down together again
> in a new rebirth of wonder . . .

Wait no longer. This rebirth of wonder starts here and now in this very moment. It begins with slowing down and observing the world as a child might, as a bright-eyed, unadulterated adult might. It's about becoming mindful and awake to the world again, filling ourselves with awe and curiosity, and finding the outlet for expressing that awe and wonder in language. Slowing down and getting quiet is key. Start by breathing in silence and see what arises within you. You'll be amazed. Meditation is such an incredible ground for writing because it's a natural reset. Given all the plans and appointments we encounter in our days—the obligations, deadlines, and desires—our mind becomes incredibly busy. Poetry and meditation allow us to settle back into our natural state of calm and open receptivity. One can only think of how a snow globe, when shaken (with blizzards of thought), blurs the scene, and then upon setting it down on a calm shelf the scene is restored to its original clarity. Well, it's just like that with thoughts, emotions, and words. They might swirl about in a chaotic mix, but once you allow them to settle, you'll find calm and clarity, which instigates an opening for your creativity and insight to blossom.

Poetry will help your writing flower no matter your genre of preference. Below you will find a meditation exercise and a writing exercise to get you started. Listen carefully to how "this April sunset completely utters" against the "prostitute Night arguing with certain houses." Remember: there is never any right or wrong in meditation, poetry, and song. So let's get started. Now is your time to reawaken the poet/writer within; now is your time to shine!

→ *A Poetry Meditation*

Begin by finding a quiet and comfortable place in your house to sit. Keep your posture upright and alert but relaxed. Read "The Snow Man" by Wallace Stevens out loud to yourself (or listen to the audio recording).

> One must have a mind of winter
> To regard the frost and the boughs
> Of the pine-trees crusted with snow;
>
> And have been cold a long time
> To behold the junipers shagged with ice,
> The spruces rough in the distant glitter
>
> Of the January sun; and not to think
> Of any misery in the sound of the wind,
> In the sound of a few leaves,
>
> Which is the sound of the land
> Full of the same wind
> That is blowing in the same bare place
>
> For the listener, who listens in the snow,
> And, nothing himself, beholds
> Nothing that is not there and the nothing that is.

Now, close your eyes and take a deep breath. Ground yourself in this moment in your body. Breathe into your experience of sitting in your body right now. Let the words echo softly, wash through you, and then let them go. There is nothing to understand or figure out. Feel into where your body makes contact with the chair or cushion. After the first deep breath, let your breathing become natural, keeping your attention with your experience of your breathing body in this position. Notice where you physically experience the breath in your body and simply bring your awareness to this experience of your breathing body. Breathe in, breathe out.

After a couple of minutes you may find your mind wandering toward plans and dreams for the future, fantasies, memories, voices of doubt or worry, excitement, joy, or other waves of emotion. That's fine—it's what minds do. As you notice whatever arises, take the opportunity to bring your attention back to your experience of your breathing body. Bring your attention back to the "listener who listens in the snow . . . to the nothing that is not there and the nothing that is."

Continue to breathe in and breathe out, allowing thoughts to be thoughts, sensations to be sensations, knowing there is nothing you need to do right now in this moment. There is nothing to get right or figure out or perfect or even understand. You are simply being in place, sitting here embodied—breathing in, breathing out, and letting go. Witnessing your experience like this, you resemble the Buddha sitting under the tree of awakening. You are waking up to the reality of the present moment, listening to the words of the poem wash through your being. You have taken on the mind of winter. Again, you are "the listener, who listens in the snow,/And, nothing himself [or herself], beholds/Nothing that is not there and the nothing that is."

To complete the meditation, take a deep breath inward and exhale slowly. Listen to the sound of the bell. When you are ready, open your eyes.

→ *A Poetry Writing Exercise: A Letter Poem Using Personification*

Start by jotting down three specific shades or hues of color, preferably colors with interesting names (for example: olive, charcoal, magenta). Look around your environment and pay attention to what you see. Then write the first three vivid verbs or strong action words that come to mind (spiraling, screeching, plowing).

Listen to the sounds around you. Then jot down three specific words for the sounds (whisper, echo, clang).

Now jot down the names of three textures or materials (cement, burlap, silk).

Now think of a "heart" emotion—the name of a feeling you would like to write a letter to. Examples include love, fear, anger, or loneliness. Note: don't choose a body feeling such as hunger or cold. Begin with "Dear _____" and then use the words you have collected so far as a launching point to write a letter to your emotion. Address it as you might a great aunt, wise friend, or deceitful neighbor. Whomever you choose, make sure to write in letter form.

Break up your sentences into lines. Include one line that has a single word and one that has ten words or more. Divide your text into at least two stanzas. Use at least one metaphor or simile. Play with slant rhyme or off rhyme; don't simply rhyme the words at the ends of your lines. Use the questions and suggestions below to prompt your writing. Have fun!

- If you could corner love in a room, what would you ask of love? Describe the room.

- If you were trapped with anger in a room, what would you ask of anger? Describe the room's shape and decorations.

- Imagine that emotion arises within you like a flower. What does that flower look like? What color? What type?

- Where in your body do you experience this emotion?
  What vivid verbs could you use to describe the movement
  or action of this feeling within you?

- If your emotion were a specific landscape, what would it be?
  Describe and name the specific features.

- If your emotion were a creature, which creature would it
  be? Describe.

- If your emotion were a character, what would they wear?
  Describe their tattoos, skin, eye color, hair, and hands.

- In addition to creating line breaks, play with the shape of
  your poem on the page.

# 5

# May
## {Imagination}

### *The Art of the Image*

Activating our imagination is about merging with the one—the mysterious one, the one that makes the imagination possible. It's about going from individuation to collective, collaborative immersion within a vast unified field of invention. Ursula Le Guin says, "Imagination, working at full strength, can shake us out of our fatal, adoring self-absorption." And I say, it does so right back into that great unified field of possibility. Whether we are writing a poem, telling the story of our life, scripting a TV show, teaching kids poetry, or imagining our way through the next great American novel, true imaginative exploration via expression saves us from the swarms of deadly ego temptation and attachment. Activation and cultivation of the imagination is a practice. Wildness is its breeding ground—wildness of place, wildness of heart and mind—love and beauty is its guiding song.

*

One foggy May morning several years ago, I was teaching at an elementary school in Northern California, at a particularly early hour, with the primary teacher out sick. There was a sub. She was awkward and nervous, with baggy skin and droopy eyes. Kids can be insensitive and even cruel, and I have unfortunately seen them pounce on adult insecurities. A room full of antsy fifth or sixth graders jacked on sugar-frosted cornflakes can render a sub helpless, especially if they lack confidence, are sleep-deprived, or come across as reactive. At worst, the sub quickly sinks, as if they were lost at sea, separated from the raft, treading water and bleeding out into shark-infested waters.

It was before eight in the morning. (Are kids even meant to be up at that hour and made to sit still?) The kids were squirming, and the boys outnumbered the girls. Not a good scenario for the visiting "poet guy." A nervous clump of dread throbbed in my stomach. The boys looked as if they were ready to rise up and commandeer the class, dragging the girls reluctantly along. I could see them looking for an opening—chattering, shifting in their chairs, loudly crumpling paper, assembling their arsenals of spitballs and tightly compressed paper grenades.

After a painfully awkward and much-interrupted introduction from the sub, I stepped forward. I startled myself with a nervously loud first couple of words. Something that might normally sound bland and ordinary ("Hi! I'm Albert, and I'm a poet!") came out overly vulnerable and weird to me, as if I had said, "Hi! I'm Albert, and I'm an alcoholic!" (which I might have, in a different context). The room became surprisingly quiet. The kids looked at me as if I had just stepped off a spaceship with green coils sprouting from my head. I was convinced they'd never even heard the word *poet* before. Their faces stared back with pure bafflement. Somehow I was able to launch into my spiel. I waved at them with both arms, as if calming an angry crowd, slowly lowering my voice and telling them how happy I was to meet them, how happy I was to *learn from them*. Learn from them? Their faces torqued in question. Undaunted, I continued. "Let's switch roles. Today, you are all the teachers and I'm your student." More silence and blank looks. I kept going. "You are the experts of your own direct sensory experience." Huh? Their heads all turned slightly to the side like a pack of curious terriers alarmed by a sharp noise in the brush. "You were all born with vast, brilliant, beautiful hearts and minds filled with complex feelings, with wild imaginations!" I was cruising now; I raised my voice. "Your heart is filled with stories that need to be heard!" *Really?* They looked perplexed, but intrigued. "I'm here because poetry is an awesome way to share those feelings and stories. I'm here to listen to you!" I could hear the symphonic music of my motivational soundtrack coming to a climax in the background. *Seriously? I thought you were here to fill my head with random factoids that have little to do with my daily fourth-grade experience.* "Each one of you is an imaginative creative genius!" I proclaimed, and I swear I heard several of them gasp. "Let's get started."

I launched into a lesson about metaphor and how a metaphor is basically a comparison between two unlike things—a way to bridge unexpected relationships among things in the world. Like a potato chip and a cloud, or, say, a tulip and a pitchfork. They still looked slightly confused, but more engaged. I used one of my favorite examples: "The red setting sun looks like . . . what? What comes to mind?" I asked, turning to face the whiteboard (*Never turn your back on the class!* I heard my mentor scold). I drew a terribly faded picture of the sun with the dried-up dry-erase marker. One of the boys in the back row (with several crumpled paper grenades at the ready) blurted out, "A blob of ketchup slipping off a wet plate?" I had to refrain from shrieking with joy. "Yes!" I boomed. "That's exactly it! Write that down!" I think I jumped a few inches off the ground. "Wow, perfect! Can't you just see that in your mind's eye, everyone?" They could. And even if they couldn't, they could feel its imaginative power in their spongy little fourth-grade bones. "That's the imagination at work." The boy beamed, and the class collectively became eager for more. Their faces all suddenly seemed to say, *Now that you mention it, I* do *have something to say. Give me a piece of paper now!*

This is who we are. Imaginative beings waking up to our creative potential, filled with unexpected ideas that are just waiting for the right spark, the right example. Sometimes all it takes is a little reminding to reconnect with that imaginative fourth grader within.

✳

Springtime in the heart of May is a time of renewal and discovery, a time of reminding, reconnecting, and remembering our true imaginative potential. Mother may I? Yes, you May. Express your full imaginative self, just as the flowers, fourth graders, and fully feathered birds do.

In this chapter, I invite you to explore a little about what the imagination actually is. I'll provide you with some fun examples from a few extraordinary young writers, touch on the hallmarks of what constitutes imaginative writing, and then zero in on a few steps you can take to jump-start or reignite your own writing more imaginatively.

*

Any proper chapter on the imagination should begin with a discussion of the *image*—the root of the word *imagination*. In the late 1980s/early '90s when I studied art at the University of Colorado, I was introduced to the writings of Suzi Gablik, a major critic in the visual art world at the time. She wrote a fascinating book called *The Reenchantment of Art* that I loved, as well as a stunning collection of interviews with major artists, critics, and cultural thinkers called *Conversations Before the End of Time*. I was floored by that title. Time is ending? It kind of felt like that to me—not only time but also all of humanity. Remember, this was between the Gulf War and the AIDS crisis, which hit the visual art world particularly hard. It felt like the whole world was, in fact, ending. I suppose every generation feels like that, given all our wars, environmental catastrophes, droughts, famines, incompetent and dangerous leaders, terrorist threats, and so on.

I have carried *Conversations Before the End of Time* with me everywhere for more than twenty years, quoting from it almost every time I teach. The book is faded, its spine is cracked, and the pages are dogeared and underlined—in red. I *never* underline books in red, unless they are incredibly special to me. Until writing these past couple of sentences, I had almost forgotten how important the book is to me, and how it shaped and nourished my thinking, writing, and teaching all these years. Thank you, Suzi!

Of all the amazing interviews in the book, there's one in particular that sticks with me. It's with David Plante, a writer I'd never heard of. His discussion with Gablik revolves around the miraculous nature of images in writing. At one point she asks him (as a writer and artist), "Are you saying that the important thing is to see the world at that moment as if from the room's or from the landscape's point of view, or what?" What a terrific question! Here's how he answers:

> Well, you try to keep yourself out of it as much as possible.
> You try to see it in its details . . . I see it in terms of details,
> telling details. Of course, the master of that is Chekhov.
> For example in a description of a room where a murder
> has taken place, he creates the space completely by having
> a bowl of boiled potatoes fall off the table into a puddle
> of blood on the floor. So you've got these white potatoes
> absorbing the blood. It's an amazing image. Even more than
> details what I have in mind is images. Chekhov might create
> a room by describing it all rather banally or simply and then
> find one image—for example, an old pair of shoes tied in a
> handkerchief—which fills the space with something that's
> impossible to qualify. In the end, I believe that writing, as all
> art, is something you can't talk about. You can't define it. I
> think writing has to defy definition.

Remember our discussion of poetry? Do I hear an echo, echo, echooo? Plante goes on:

> An image that occurs in writing is closer to the mystery of
> awareness to me than an image you actually see with your
> eyes. Images that occur when you close your eyes are very
> mysterious things and don't relate, except perhaps in common
> parlance, to what we see when our eyes are open . . . the
> image itself is a miracle. And images are miracles because we
> don't know how they are produced . . . images are miracles. I
> believe that paintings are miracles. Sculpture, photographs,

and films are miracles. But the miracle that most inspires me is the miracle of an image in a poem or play or novel. We are inspired by miracles not in terms of what they intend, not in terms of any dogmas or definitions or commentary they support, but in terms of an awareness of something greater than what we ourselves can do.

This is the essence of writing as a path to awakening, which is about accessing and connecting into the miraculous nature of our endeavors. Can we embody that drive, that impulse, that experience of the miraculous in writing? When we start to see art, art making, and therefore life making as miracles, as sacred, we are living the path of awakening. We can then proactively act from beauty, generosity, and love rather than reacting from conditioned thought and knee-jerk emotional drives.

Where does an image (a thought) come from? We don't know. That not-knowing immediately qualifies as a luscious mystery, if not a miracle. We don't know how an image is created, and it's precisely that enigma that makes it miraculous. Being in awe of the miraculous is our spiritual home base—the place to begin from, and return to, often.

*

Can you locate your imagination in time and space? Does it emanate from an orange shaft of sunlight angling in the corner of your eye at dusk? Is it perched somewhere in your head like a box full of tangled wires? Does it live within the depths of your body, packed in around the honeycomb wilderness of your bones, strewn about the sinewy freeway of your left elbow? Is it sizzling at a pinpoint prick of starlight forty-seven million light-years above the intersection of Hollywood and Vine? Blocked out by steely blue clouds forming a two-hundred-miles-per-hour wind funnel funneling up the town of Tonganoxie, Kansas? Perhaps your imagination is right now passing through the melodious background twitter of a cedar waxwing, or hidden underneath the tough echo of your mother's dying voice.

All and none of the above. Trying to define the imagination or even locate it is futile. Limiting something so gorgeous and mysterious, something so much like a lilac nebula of stars, to mere definition seems not only futile but also inane. At some level, we know we all have an imagination deep within; we know that it's something we were born with. So the question becomes more about exploration and investigation, about tapping into this brilliant and innate aspect of the self. Really, my intent here is to help move you toward realizing your part in this cosmic imaginative play. I want to create a glint of hope that crackles into a fervor of possibility, eventually erupting into a firestorm of passion in which *you* take action, tapping into that vast dappled explosion of stars spinning in your bloodstream this very instant. I want you to write, write, write—your way to beauty, insight, and wholeness.

**TRY THIS**  Write down a few images right now in this moment. An image isn't only visual, it's also sensory. What are a few simple things you notice? Take a moment to settle into your sensory experience. Bring your awareness to the simple act of seeing. What colors, shapes, or specific details can you notice and name before you? Simply write down what you see. Now switch to hearing. What are you hearing in this moment? Describe sounds nearby and far away. How about smells? Tastes? What lingering sensation rests on your tongue from your most recent meal? Bring your awareness to your skin—a specific place on your body, the insistent textures from the slightest itch to a dramatic abrasion—what can you compare that sensation to?

To further inspire your imagination, I thought about offering some images from my favorite imaginative writers (Emily Dickinson, Hildegard of Bingen, Richard Brautigan, Federico García Lorca, Toni Morrison, among many others), but then I thought it best to share a couple of examples from students—the kids I met while working with California Poets in the Schools. Who better to illustrate our innate, extraordinary brilliance? As I tell these students, everyone comes into this human form with an imagination and the capacity to create, invent, and express their truth. The amazing poet and teacher June Jordan defines poetry (writing) as "a medium for telling the truth." And so, our plan here is to explore the universe of our heart and mind. My job is to ask kids (and you): *Who are you? What are your dreams?* What do you think and feel about the galaxy, the world, your parents, your peers, yourself, history, animals, the environment? What happens when you express those thoughts and feelings through the unfettered and unlimited medium of words?

Masumi Taketomi, a student at La Jolla High School, writes: "My sister is the winter moon . . . She guides me through the crumbling moss of nightmares." Wow! That's the power of pure, unadulterated imagination at work. It's beyond definition, description, explanation, or even meaning. "Out beyond ideas of wrongdoing and rightdoing, there is a field. I'll meet you there," says Rumi. This field is your field of imaginative possibility. Check out this exposition on Sojourner Truth from eighth-grader Nico Gallyot: "A lightning bolt upon her creator's word, A mudslide through the nation of her people." See? We are everywhere. Ordinary geniuses like Nico and Masumi, like Joe, Mary, Juan, Abdul, Marina, Estelle, Albert, and you. All of us saying "yes" to allowing ourselves a moment to be imaginative, to be human.

Whether it's inventing a monster under the bed, demonizing an opposing politician, or gossiping about your neighbor who just the other day tossed her husband's pink Stratocaster off their deck in a fit of amplified rage, we can't escape our imaginative selves. Our imagination is the core essence of our cognitive being.

Given a little space and a shift of attention, your imagination comes alive to color your life with beauty and possibility. It's a question of courage, patience, and willingness to turn your attention from the seductive external world of caustic physicality to the soft internal mystery of consciousness. You are being called to delve deep into the emotional-sensorial maelstrom of awareness and see what lies beyond. This process of writing and creativity, of tapping into your imaginative self, has less to do with the questions of "Am I good enough?" "Hasn't it all been said before?" "Could I ever be as good as so and so?"

"Am I even an artistic or creative person?" and "Do I even have the time?" and more to do with the question of desire and timing. *When* will you *choose* to stop the chatter in your head and say yes? *Now* is always the time, literally. Don't wait. This is your moment to allow inspiration in and your imaginative brilliance out!

✱

What, then, are the hallmarks of a cultivated imagination? You know it when you read it, see it, taste it, touch it, smell it, feel it, or hear it. Strong imaginative writing is filled with sensory details; it's drunk on surprise, wildness, curious twists on the familiar. Imaginative writing is unrestrained, sometimes impolite, and emotionally rough around the edges as it claws its way toward truth. Consider the following from Ian McEwan's novel *The Children Act*:

> Then she looked at Jack. He stood well away from her, feet apart, arms crossed, his still-handsome, good-natured face stiff with anger. A wisp of silvery chest hair curled up through his open-necked shirt. She had sometimes seen him tease it up with a comb. That the world should be filled with such detail, such tiny points of human frailty, threatened to crush her and she had to look away.

This is the perfect example of the emotional role and ultimate impact of those tiny imaginative details. They don't just *crush* your characters emotionally; they crush your readers, too. And by "crush" I mean *expose*, *submit*, and *open* them to emotionally potent frontiers within themselves. Such imaginative writing is sometimes obnoxious in this regard; it can come across as exaggerated or even hyperbolic. It's corrugated, serrated, overinflated. It's peppered with green, blue, red, orange, purple, black, and white lies. *What? You're telling me to lie in my writing?* In an essay titled "Dostoevsky and Swedenborg," Czeslaw Milosz writes of the "right of the poet to invent—that is, to lie." So, in a manner of speaking, yes, lie, but never be deceitful or dishonest. Lie with the higher truths at your side. Tell a small, blond lie in order to arrive at a sumptuous and blinding lemon-yellow truth.

Kids tend to lie from a young age, partly to test the boundaries of physical reality (gravity, speed, the limits of their bodies in relationship to these forces) and partly in reaction to the reality presented to them by adults. They often lie out of ignorance; they get the information wrong. They don't mean any harm. They are generally not yet perceptive or facile enough with language to report an incident with complete accuracy, and they are navigating their way through language to see what works in terms of understanding, as well as power, social positioning, status, etc. This fits in perfectly with a healthy imagination. Stories without some hyperbole, lies, half-truths, deception, drama, and a hefty heaping of clashing desire don't tend to interest us. Two people with conflicting motives will use the immediacy of their language to manipulate a situation to their specific end—you'll find this tendency at the core of high drama in theater, film, and fiction. With kids, lying is largely okay up until a certain age, when we expect (hope) they will mature to socially acceptable beings who don't manipulate or thieve their way through life.

Oscar Wilde once said, "Lying, the telling of beautiful untrue things, is the proper aim of Art." So telling wondrous untruths is part of the writing process; it's our natural inclination to use language as a lever to find higher truth, even if that means "stretching the truth." Again, one needs to be careful here. There's an enormous difference between lying consciously and stretching a "lower" truth to reach a "higher" truth in the name of art. To be clear, what I'm advocating has nothing to do with manipulating others or avoiding responsibility for your actions, and everything to do with staying true to your emotional intent while being honest with your readers.

In addition to sensory detail, specificity, and hyperbole, another hallmark of imaginative writing is its fresh, edgy, even rogue nature that ranges far beyond a simple chronicle or listing of facts. You are free (and encouraged) to stumble about and pick through the colorful garbage of reportage on your way to the forest-spooky wilderness of imaginative collage. Imaginative writing is messy and inaccurate the way the poppy flower in my garden is, with its hopelessly fragile tissue-torn petals pummeled by last night's angry rain. The way its fat papery head is too big for the stalk and how it leans out beyond the garden fence, where its gauzy mustard beautifulness is bound for consumption by the next hungry passing deer. Imaginative writing exposes the bloodied underbelly and raw viscera of existence, sticking right up against its onion-skinned elegance. It begs for our mushy purple innards to be turned inside out. It ain't pretty, but it's drop-dead gorgeous. Imaginative writing asks you and your readers to squirm a little in their pews in mutual or oscillating discomfort and delight. It asks you to open up not only your senses but also your tender vulnerable heart.

*

There are a number of ways to jump-start and respark your writerly imagination. Let's begin by remembering that curiosity and imagination are primary to the human experience. Even if we were shut down in childhood by nagging social pressures, casual abuse, or even violence, we can still ignite a renaissance of the imagination in adulthood.

**Step I   Desiring desire.** You must sincerely want to reconnect with your imaginative self, to wake up and realize that you are profoundly curious about the world. You must feel that you have something interesting and imaginative to share from your unique experience, and you must yearn to say it and set it free.

**Step 2   Attending to your attention.** Cultivate your imagination by focusing your attention on writers you love, artists that move you to tears, discomfort, and delight. I also recommend spending time in nature. Contact with the nonhuman world is the wellspring of a flourishing imaginative consciousness. Next time you are out on a walk, bring your notebook. Take a moment to sit on a rock or log. Write down what you hear, see, smell, taste, and touch—be as specific as you can. Simply observe directly, and see what you come up with. There's nothing quite as imaginatively generative as the experience of crouching down in the tall grass as a coyote prances within ten feet of your body, or listening to the hollow bellow of a great horned owl beneath a midnight stand of moon-splintered redwoods. Lastly—it seems silly to even write this down, but if I've learned anything in my forty-something years on this earth it's that repetition is the key to education—write down your dreams and keep a consistent journal. Practice, practice, practice—and without petty evaluation, judgment, or self-recrimination, please. Write for the sake of seeing what you have to say, for the pure curiosity of it.

**Step 3 Surrendering to silence.** Spend time in silence every day, lest you remain caught in the chronic chatter of the world, with all its opinion-slinging and mechanical celebrations of the mundane. It can drive one crazy. At a certain point, it is essential to just stop and let it all go. Drop the pen and sit still. Stillness and silence are key to a balanced writing life. Excessive thinking and obsessing over language, images, ideas, and meaning can twist your mind into knots of confusion and despair. Letting go should be a daily practice. Some days the mind is a torrent of ideas and you can't stop accumulating pages of brilliance. Other times, nothing. Some days you might construct a single sentence or a single word and you'll feel okay with that. Perhaps one day your mind is blank, empty, or strewn with boring clichés. Go to the movies, grab a milkshake, set out on a bike ride, weed the goddamn garden, or take a bath and let it all go. Trust that the universe will fill you back up again and again and again—which it will, I promise. If you give yourself to silent meditation every day, you will never be at a loss for ideas, insights, and revelations. You will never be at a loss for peace and calm, for deep connection; you will never be separated from your imaginative genius. Yes, of course you will still experience sadness, doubt, fear, and anxiety, but over time you will become friendly with these visitors; you won't get snagged by them, and the spaciousness within you will grow to accommodate the totality of being human. Along the way, you will tap into the infinite creativity of the universe and eventually recognize it as your own true nature.

**Step 4   Practicing practice and learning to revere repetition.** Practice the cultivation of both meditative letting go and imaginative letting in on a consistent basis. Am I repeating myself? Good, and so should you—repeat yourself repeatedly. Now get cracking, if you haven't already. The writing exercises in each chapter are designed to get you to the page. Hopefully, at this point you have set the book down and are scribbling away in your journal!

For those of you who are still here reading, chewing your lip, hemming and hawing, who have never really thought of yourselves as particularly imaginative or creative people, banish that thought from your minds right now and read on—or rather *write* on. Start by tuning into the art and writing toward what you resonate with. That resonance is your guide and actually a facet of your imagination at work. It starts with appreciation and recognition and then expands into cultivation and eventually creation.

Early on in my writing career, I was so transported, so emotionally jolted by the words of Federico García Lorca (as much as I am today by such fourth-grade students as Caroline) that I immediately *knew* that I wanted to add to this exquisite conversation, that I deeply *needed* to contribute my take on the human experience as filtered through my own battered and beautiful self. At the time, I falsely believed that the artists I adored possessed rare and unobtainable gifts that were in limited supply and selectively given out by God Almighty Him- or Herself. I was convinced that I simply didn't get tapped as one of the "gifted ones." I just couldn't understand that most of my creative genius heroes and heroines had been cranking out shitty work forever until, after years of practice, revision, and rejection, some of their efforts finally started to glow with imaginative impact. Sure, there are those extremely rare birds who are born with a certain aptitude and facility in the arts, but they still have to claim it and work it—it's never a given. For the rest of us, including some of the most well-known names in literature, we must explore until something surprising flowers from within.

So remember, you *are* your imagination. It's not something outside of you that you read in the pages of some book, or something you overhear in the next booth over at Bubba's Drive-In, or even the memory of your adventures trekking across Nepal (although these are all terrific things to write about). It's found *within* you—your imaginative heart and soul, looking like a nebula of stars throbbing in your bloodstream a thousand times a second, at this very moment.

�»  *Imagination Meditation Exercise*

Here's a way to practice conjuring up (imagining) and letting go: the standing "skeleton-scan" meditation.

Find a quiet place in your house with a soft and comfortable surface to stand on. If you don't have a carpet, try using a yoga mat.

Close your eyes and take a deep breath inward. Ground yourself in this moment, in your body; breathe into your experience of standing upright. After the first deep breath, let your breathing become natural. Keep your attention with your body as it breathes in this position.

Feel your breathing in your belly. Breathe in, breathe out.

If your mind wanders, that's okay. Remember, that's what minds do. As you notice the natural flow of your thoughts, take the opportunity to bring your attention back to breathing from and into your belly. Continue to breathe in and out.

Now lightly bring a thread of your awareness to your feet and breathe into your feet. Feel the stability and grounding of your breath at your feet. See into your feet and imagine right now with your mind's eye the little toe bones of your feet, the phalanges. Follow your imagining to the main parts of your feet, the metatarsals and tarsals, to where they meet your ankle bones. See that connection at your ankles, then continue up your legs to view the tibias joining at your knees. Visualize your knees as they meet your patellae, and then see the femurs rising up to connect at your hip bones. See your hip bones where they connect to your sacrum and your spine. Now visualize your vertebrae climbing and then branching out into your rib cage. See the ribs of your body wrapping around you and joining at your sternum, protecting your heart. Notice now your clavicles and scapulae, the bones of your shoulders holding your arms, and see those bones of your upper arms. The humeri meet your elbows, and the ulnae and radiuses of your lower arms connect at your wrists. Visualize those bones of your hands, the carpals and metacarpals, the finger phalanges. Now bring your visualization back through your hands to your wrists, up your arms past your elbows, back up to your shoulders, and see now your neck and cervical vertebrae, where your spine connects to your skull. See your skull, the round smoothness of the bone with hollow sockets for your eyes and nose, and see the bones of your jaw and teeth. Breathe into this visualized experience of your skeleton. See your entire skeleton glowing in your mind's eye. Breathe in and feel your body swaying gently, knowing right now this skeleton is your stability and ground—these mineral bones, your conduit to earth and sky. Take a deep breath inward, exhale, and open your eyes.

---

→ *Imagination Writing Exercise*

Find an image of an intriguing-looking person in a favorite magazine—an anonymous model, not a known celebrity or personality—and write a brief biography of that person. Describe what you see in the picture with as much detail as possible. Imaginative writing is specific and sensory. Get down to the hairline, describe what it looks like in between their teeth, write about the buttons on their sweater and the bracelet or earrings you can't see. Do these objects have special meaning in their life? Make it up. Invent. Include the furniture, curtains, paintings in the background, cars, or any other aspects of the landscape. Include color, shape, and texture. What month is it? What sounds do you hear? If the picture is in black and white, add specific colors as you imagine them. What is this person thinking right now? What is their emotional state, their mood? Describe all this with your details. What just happened five minutes before this picture was taken? What is about to happen? Go. Don't think. Write for at least fifteen minutes, and write with fervor and passion and beyond thought. Let your imagination bloom, like a rain-drenched garden in May.

<hr />

# Summer

6

# June
## {Amusement}

*Surprise, Humor, Taking the Vow,*
*and Calling Forth the Muse*

How about some song lyrics to bring us into summer, to call forth the muse of June? I encourage you to put down this book right now, find the song "Summertime Thing" by Chuck Prophet, and crank it up loud.

> That summer heat has got me feeling lazy
> The air is warm and the sky is hazy
> People getting down, getting crazy
> People getting down, getting stupid, getting crazy
>
> Hey, it's a summertime thing
> Summertime thing

If the groove and lyrics don't amuse you and get you in a summertime mood, then put on a bathing suit, step into a pair of ratty flip-flops, wrap a brightly colored beach towel around your neck, and replay the song. How about now? Are you packing the cooler and heading to the beach, the delta, or the river? Sometimes it's necessary to dress the part before a writing session to get you amused and activated. Even if you don't like "Summertime Thing" (even if it isn't your thing), see if you can enter the amusing spirit of it.

Go ask your dad for the keys to the Honda
Can your sister come along, how could she not wanna?
Put the Beach Boys on, wanna hear "Help Me Rhonda"
Roll down the sides, we'll drive to the Delta

Imaginative writing should amuse us at some level. What does that look like? For me, it involves quirky, unexpected rhymes, altered syntax, new arrangements of language, surprising plot twists, strange settings, or unusual characters. In "The Business of Writing Poetry," Ted Berrigan says, "There's only one way essentially to write poems [songs, novels, memoirs, etc.] that are no good. And that's to be not very amusing. And so don't do that, don't be *un*amusing." Let this be our summertime thing—in addition to writing imaginatively, we'll aim to be amusing.

The poet Frank O'Hara considered the whole enterprise of writing to be, at times, a form of amusing oneself first, and *then* (hopefully) the reader as he riffs off overheard conversations, makes up strange and funny word combinations, absurdly contradicts himself, or simply expresses a goofy thought while strolling the moody summertime streets of Manhattan. In "All That Gas," O'Hara writes, "I am walking along the sidewalk and I see a puddle and it's god, greedy god, always adding to yourself with raindrops and spit...." I love how O'Hara sneaks in this rather simple yet spiritually profound comment to god in the otherwise mundane act of walking the streets.

What does it mean to be amusing, not only for our writing but also for the entirety of our being? Let's take *amusement* both literally and metaphorically. There is a whole genre of satirists and humor writers, and some people are just born funny. Isn't a good sense of humor in some way genetic? Certain people seem to grow up with funny parents and it rubs off on them. Most people wouldn't describe me as a funny person, but they might describe me as someone with a good sense of humor, if only because I laugh a lot, love a good joke, and can often see the hilarious in the otherwise dark and tragic. Like writing, effective humor is subtle, nuanced, and sometimes highly practiced. It's never just the content of the joke—humor involves context, pacing, and tone. I would say that you need colorful or animated speech to tell a good joke, but then I remember the comedian Steven Wright, who has made an entire career of reciting absurdities in a flat-faced monotone ("If toast always lands butter-side down, and cats always land on their feet, what happens if you strap toast on the back of a cat and drop it?").

> **TRY THIS**  Write your own amusing song. Take a look at some of your favorite songs and see how they work as poems. The renowned songwriter Townes Van Zandt once said that a song needs to first work as a poem. Look at classic rhyming poems such as William Blake's famous poem "The Tyger": "Tyger, tyger, burning bright,/In the forests of the night,/What immortal hand or eye,/Could frame thy fearful symmetry?" Of course, you have to pronounce the word *symmetry* so that it rhymes with eye, but there's amusement for you. Use rhyme as your guide. Get goofy and have fun.

My mother told her favorite joke with a vivacious drunken enthusiasm; her dynamic gestures and voicing made it hard to resist: "What's Irish and stays outside all year round?" she loudly blurted in her crummy Irish accent (she was from Boston). "Patty O'Furniture." That joke slays me every time. Probably because I associate it with my mother and can see her swaying about in the kitchen with a "ciggie" in one hand and a martini in the other, saying for the third or fourth time, "Darling, darling, I have the most cunning joke for you . . ." Amusement by memory and association. Much of what's funny in writing and performance is context, association, situation, and, of course, personal perception and preference. Don't most of our revered comedians look so natural and at ease on stage? And yet the more you learn about their routine and the more you study their habits, you find out just how nervous or terrified, even depressed, they are. You discover how they actually rehearse the same jokes over and over again, hundreds of times. Comics are writers and disciplined practitioners first, performers second, and great amusers third.

When I arrived at art school in the early 1990s, I had no idea what I was doing. Even though I had a BFA degree in photography from the University of Colorado, had taken some interesting photographs while traveling abroad in Africa, and had somehow weaseled my way into the graduate program at the San Francisco Art Institute, I was just twenty-five and pretty much lost to the big city. I was still reeling from a messy, abusive, and alcoholic adolescence, and I was clueless regarding creative discipline and hard work. The administration and instructors assumed that, as a graduate student, you had your routine, your habits, and some sense of clarity about the trajectory and momentum of your work. Nothing could have been further from the truth for me. I only worked part-time gigs off and on for a little spending money, because my guilt-ridden father insisted on paying for my housing and tuition. Who was I to argue? (Even though relying on his support resulted in stunting my self-esteem and sense of independence.) Given the simple task of making art between occasional readings and gallery viewing assignments, I still felt overwhelmed and bewildered. And during our critique sessions when the other students would talk about the "derisive formulaic use of the color wheel" or "Wittgenstein's logical thought-form propositions," I felt confused and stupid. They may as well have been speaking Urdu.

In the art world at the time, everyone seemed to be making balls of one kind or another: Ann Hamilton and her balls of horsehair, David Ireland and his balls of cement, James Lee Byars and his balls of gold. So I thought, *I too shall make my profound art ball.* Sitting in my cramped studio in the Haight, eating a corner-store tuna sandwich one day, I absentmindedly crumpled up its aluminum foil wrapper into a shiny, tuna-stained ball. I stared at it. The metallic golf ball–sized orb stared back. It glowed. It radiated and beamed at me like an oracle. It spoke to me, told me it wanted to be held and nurtured, and announced that it yearned to evolve into a mature grown-up ball of aluminum foil. I listened carefully, as if encouraging an unpredictable and moody child. I grabbed a roll of aluminum foil from my so-called kitchen and added to my now adolescent-sized art-child. Then I ran down to Lucky's in the Mission and bought ten rolls of industrial-sized aluminum foil.

My ball grew and grew until I could no longer fit it through the door of my apartment. So I took the door off its hinges, smushed the ball through, and rolled it out onto the sidewalk and down the street. We went everywhere together, me and my enormous ball of aluminum foil. It became a character in the imaginary art movie of my life. I photographed it rolling through the grass in Golden Gate Park, and perched it on the seawall at Ocean Beach, where it hovered on the horizon above the ocean like a slowly rising metallic planet. I placed it on sidewalks with people watching it, and photographed them together sharing tentative space. For a second, I felt like a deep and profound artist. I was like John Malkovich in *Art School Confidential*, where he's at an opening for his "new" triangle paintings, and he says pompously to a baffled student next to him, "You know, I invented triangles." I was like that for a brief period of time. In a self-congratulatory voice of exquisite seriousness, I whispered to myself in the mirror, "You know, *you* invented art balls."

\*

Once upon a time, two literalists who also happened to be hunters were strolling down a logging road in remotest Oregon wearing plaid shirts, khaki cargo shorts, gray wool socks, and clunky leather hiking boots. They had binoculars around their necks, wide-brimmed sun hats, and small backpacks strapped to their backs. They strode along with shiny guns slung over their shoulders. I'm pretty sure they were whistling "God Bless America." Until they came to a fork in the road with a sign that read "bear left," so they went home.

Humor is sometimes simple, dumb, and goofy; sometimes it's odd and compelling; sometimes it's absurd and inappropriately hilarious. Regardless, the key to being amusing in our writing is to practice being amusing without *trying* to be amusing. I'm not sure what your experience is, but whenever I *try* to be funny, I'm usually not (see above). And since you may not have found my joke funny, I'll quote someone who is more verifiably amusing than I. Here's David Sedaris on overcoming writers block from an AMA ("Ask Me Anything") event on Reddit:

Sometimes when I'm stuck, I'll open an English textbook, and do the homework.

There are a lot of college writing textbooks that will include essays and short stories, and after reading the story or essay, there will be questions such as "Have YOU had any experience with a pedophile in YOUR family?" or "When was the last time you saw YOUR mother drunk?" and they're just really good at prompting stories. You answer the question, and sometimes that can spring into a story.

Sedaris is making a joke. Sort of. Far too many of us *can* write about the last time we saw our mothers drunk. Sometimes it becomes the basis for our memoir. Sometimes she becomes the protagonist in our novel.

*

*A-muse-ment.* If we break the word down, it means "courting the muse." In other words, allowing inspiration and insight to flow through you. My first book of poetry, *Letters to Early Street*, began as a series of epistolary updates to a dear friend I quietly considered my muse. In our culture, the traditional muse is often portrayed in movies as some beautiful young woman who drives a young man mad with lusty creativity. In actuality, a muse can exist as any person (living or dead) who inspires you to sit down and do the hard work of writing. For me, it was my friend Demian, a passionate playwright and poet who shared my enthusiasm for Spanish poets such as Federico García Lorca, Juan Ramón Jiménez, and Antonio Machado. Demian and I used to get together regularly, talking manically about other writers we loved over twenty-seven cups of coffee, sometimes staying up all night encouraging, challenging, and pushing each other to write.

I recently read about an author who begins each writing session by invoking *the* muse—that is, the original Greek muse—from Homer's *Odyssey*. This writer actually reads the classic invocation at the beginning of Book One of *The Odyssey* that begins "O Divine

Poesy, goddess, daughter of Zeus, sustain for me this song . . ." as if alerting the gods and goddesses to guide him in his writing and allow the creative energies to flow. It's a prayer, a song, a cry for guidance and support on the journey through resistance, doubt, and difficulty into the gilded gateway of divine creativity. I love this idea. When I started typing it up for myself, I found the translation too archaic (no matter how timeless), so I felt inspired to write my own updated version. I figured doing so would resonate and energize me more. Here's my rendition:

### O Divine Poesy, O Great Muse

Please bring forth for me insight and beauty,
the tiny and the infinite energies of the gods and goddesses,
animal and mineral spirits, cosmic forces from the spring of
creation . . .

Sustain for me this eternal song as gift,
in this moment as is eternity, let me be a vessel for goodness—
may my heart in its time remain open, creative, vulnerable,
bright, and true—
please let all the temptations, resistances, and distractions
retreat in your wake, allowing
the flow of thought, idea, language to burn brightly
through me and beyond me, back unto you . . .
casting both shadows and yet clearer beams
of love, insight, and revelation
upon the readers and seers, hearers as well as those silent and
blind . . .

May the work that comes through this temporal vessel
be blessed by these energies for the goodness
of all human, all animal, all entities between and beyond
and throughout universal time.
With gratitude, surrender, humility, and grace . . .
and forever in love.

For the record, here's Homer's version as translated by T. E. Lawrence (Lawrence of Arabia):

> O Divine Poesy
> Goddess-daughter of Zeus
> Sustain for me
> This song of the various-minded man,
> Who after he had plundered
> The innermost citadel of hallowed Troy
> Was made to stray grievously
> About the coasts of men,
> The sport of their customs good or bad,
> While his heart
> Through all the seafaring
> Ached in an agony to redeem himself
> And bring his company safe home
>
> Vain hope—for them!
> For his fellows he strove in vain,
> Their own witlessness cast them away;
> The fools,
> To destroy for meat
> The oxen of the most exalted sun!
> Wherefore the sun-god blotted out
> The day of their return.
>
> Make the tale live for us
> In all its many bearings,
> O Muse.

*

Speaking of muses, Ted Berrigan used to refer to writers who "got you to the page." He was talking about writers who inspire you so much that you'll stop reading their words to suddenly jot down a few of your own. For this reason, I always read with a notebook by my side. Sometime it's just to copy down an amazing quote, but sometimes a scene will inspire a new story line, concept, or creative trajectory for me. We all have favorite writers who simply *inspire* us—we are captivated by their ideas, style, and use of language to such an extent that we also want to share our unique voice with the world. These writers move us beyond mere appreciation into *participation*—they invite us in and encourage us to contribute. In the presence of their work and enduring spirit, our blocks are lifted, comparisons with their work fall away, and we receive their permission to write from our true center. This process is another way the muse can speak through us.

> **TRY THIS** Make a list of ten writers who get you to the page. Reread them. Remind yourself why you love these authors—what specifically about their work drives you to want to create. And it doesn't have to be writers you necessarily like, but those who inspire you to pick up the pen and go. Maybe your list includes "marginal" writers—those you consider less than great or people who inspire the thought, "Dang, I could do better than that!" Consider these writers your muses.

Writing should ultimately be fun and funny. Life is too short to take ourselves too seriously, and it's definitely too short to get caught up in the struggles and anguish of the creative act. We'll face plenty of challenges along the way. Why not begin each day by invoking the muse, by laughing a little at the absurdity of the whole beautifully crazy endeavor of living the creative life?

We want the muse to infiltrate, titillate, and propagate within us. Amusement is full engagement, full entertainment. Occasionally I venture off to Lake Tahoe by myself for some intensive and uninterrupted writing time. I make a vow to wake up at six (at the latest) and not leave my room until noon (at the earliest). One day I simply hit the wall. Just after nine, I had absolutely nothing more to write. I paced around my room, I scribbled crap in my notebook, obsessively fondled its pages, and I read. I reread. I surfed the Internet, pored over forest service maps, and planned hikes and bike rides. I stared at the clock, willing its hands forward. Most of all, I sat around feeling guilty for even thinking about bailing early. Finally I just threw in the towel. I went on a short hike, then a mountain bike ride, and ate a nice lunch at an outdoor café, listening in on conversations at nearby tables. I walked to the library and chatted with the librarian about local lore. I perused the local bookstore. Basically, I went *out* to get amused. I eventually found my way back to my little room, sat right down to meditate, and went *inside* to amuse the amuser—to awaken my internal muse. What did I find? Goofiness, humor, surprises, and, by the next day, an infinite river of words and ideas that spilled forth from the muse itself.

→ *Laughing Meditation/Yoga Exercise*

Lie down flat on your back. Fully extend your body on a yoga mat or comfortable surface. Close your eyes and take a deep breath inward. Exhale. Take a second deep breath and exhale slowly. Take a third. Keep your eyes closed gently and just tune into the rhythm of your breathing. Breathe regularly and notice your breath moving in and out.

Now pay attention to your body as it relaxes into the floor, into the earth. If you feel obvious points of tension, breathe into those areas of your body and let them relax. Let your head and neck relax, drop your shoulders, let your back and hips sink into the floor, and rest your arms softly at your sides. Continue to breathe naturally as your legs and feet relax into the floor. You might bring your attention now to wherever you experience your breath in your body. And when your mind begins to explore one topic or the other, just gently call it back to paying attention to your breath, to your body.

Now, bring your knees up to your chest and wrap your arms around them. Slowly rock back and forth. Smile. Even if it's forced, exaggerate your smile. Turn your beaming face up to the sky.

Continue to rock back and forth slowly and breathe deep from your belly. Now I'd like you to laugh, beginning with deep "ho, ho, ho" sounds from your belly on the exhale, then adding "ha, ha, ha" when you inhale. Alternate back and forth like that, exaggerating more loudly with each breath. Try doing this until you are naturally laughing from the absurdity of it all. See if you can rock and laugh yourself into hysterics for ten or twenty minutes, or at least until the laughter fades.

Close your eyes and take a deep breath. Check in with the sensations coursing through your body. Offer gratitude as you enjoy the release of tension, increased relaxation, and sensations of peace. Open your eyes to conclude the meditation.

*Note: You can do this meditation by yourself, but there's nothing like sharing it with three or more people. A small group offers a delightful exchange of amusement energy.*

---

### (A) Muse (Ment) Writing Exercise

Write your invocation to the muse as a poem, prayer, or chant. You can base it on Homer's classic form or simply make up your own. How would your version read? What other invocation or prayer could you employ to get you to the page and sustain you through the storms of resistance and distraction that will inevitably assail you at times when you tentatively approach your writing? Take time to play with this idea. Create your own invocation, your own holy creativity prayer. See what happens. Write it, edit it, and polish it until it resonates deeply within you. Write something with heart and depth that you will want to type up and even frame. Place it on your altar or stick it to your computer so it will inspire great writing from and through you!

Then sing it loud and proud before every writing session, and behold as your writing beams with creative brilliance, ease, and grace.

---

# 7

# July
## {Audacity}

*Absolute Daring . . . Telling/Writing the Truth*

To prepare for the dog days of summer, we move from amusement to audacity. Being a dog owner and lover, I particularly enjoy the expression "dog days." I always picture a pile of lazy dogs panting away in the shade of a chestnut tree, waiting out the heat of the day to go for an evening walk. Venturing into the heat of creative and spiritual practice takes courage; it is an audacious undertaking.

Writing and meditation are acts of courage because they both require a sincere (and sometimes brutally honest) confrontation with the self. We might not regularly associate audacity with meditation and spirituality, although maybe more so with writing, which asks us to not only create but also to *share*, so there's perhaps a little more exposure involved. When it comes to meditation, what could be more simple than sitting down, being quiet, and breathing? It turns out that for most people, meditation can prove an incredible challenge. For some, it's a real terror.

When you sit down to meditate for the first time, it can be quite uncomfortable. You see just how active and tangential the mind can be. Unexpected emotions can arise for seemingly no apparent reason. You may even feel confronted by strong fear and uncertainty. For those of us who are so conditioned with constant stimulation, the pure boredom of meditation can prove agonizing. In other words, showing up fully for this moment is an audacious act. In fact, it's a radical act.

Writing as a path to awakening invites you to go ahead—be wild, be bold, be brave. Be an example of intrepid daring. I dare you. To be audacious means to redefine yourself as a person of courage, as a writer of boldness, as someone who is willing to show up with full vulnerability and presence. Time to step forward and present your ideas to the world; communicate that which you truly believe with conviction and compassion. Some of us may not even know what we want to say. Meditation can provide the space for questions to arise, for ideas to crop up, for energy to build, for intention to become clear, and for confusion to dissolve.

To me, the word *audacity* connotes sassiness. Or is it gumption? A hands-on-hips stance that proclaims, "Hey, listen up. I've got something to tell you." If you're like me, you might occasionally (or regularly) hear another voice—more persistent, less supportive. It mumbles, "But who am I? What do I have to add to the conversation? Who am I to think I can bring anything new or interesting to the table?" The appropriately audacious response is, "Who are you to think you *can't?*" As writer and spiritual teacher Marianne Williamson so eloquently reminds us in *A Return to Love*, "Your playing small does not serve the world."

Audacity requires courage. It means feeling your fear and doing it (whatever it is that scares you) anyway! It means moving beyond timidity, safety, and the habits that keep us hiding out in our small, familiar worlds. Audacity requires a quest into the dark hollows of the unknown. Every act of placing pen to paper and facing the cold open tundra of the page is an act of strength and courage, an example of daring. When you put yourself out there—your ideas, beliefs, dreams, hopes, ideas—you become vulnerable and exposed; you open yourself to scrutiny, strong opinions (sometimes informed, but mostly uninformed), and even harsh judgment and dismissal. This is the deal we make with audacity: When we meet life audaciously, we meet it open-heartedly. We willingly expose ourselves to the epic beauties and devastating hurts of life.

I recently interviewed the wonderful writer Elizabeth Gilbert. I found it inconceivable that she sometimes comes across vitriolic and hateful comments about her work. How can it be that someone of such exceptional kindness and insight—someone who has devoted her life to creativity and connection, who constantly works to build a more inclusive and generous society—is dismissed or ridiculed? I don't understand haters like this, other than to guess that they're blinded by woundedness or ignorance. Personally, I don't think a critic's opinion holds any weight unless they're out there being audacious themselves (which is rarely the case).

Anyway, back to you, dear reader. I want you to be courageous and bold; I want you to be audacious. As my friend Tim would implore, take on a "BHAG"—a Big, Hairy, Audacious Goal. Write forth your truth and wake up to expanded awareness in the process. Whether that means starting a journal or writing a poem, novel, memoir, or letter to your grandmother—audacity will drive you forward. I want you to commit here and now to do your best in any given moment. Move forward with your best intentions of creativity and spiritual awakening at heart.

✳

For as long as I can remember, I have been moved and inspired by speakers. Although the prospect of speaking before a giant audience has always terrified me, I've always wanted to do it. A large percentage of people would rather die than speak in public. Literally. According to several oft-repeated surveys, public speaking ranks up there with death as one of people's most intense fears. An academic survey from 2015 found that 30 percent of the fifteen hundred people polled named public speaking as one of their major fears. Obamacare, reptiles, and zombies (at 8 percent) also ranked notably high. I learned a few things from this survey: first, don't believe everything you read on the Internet; second, I share a fear of public speaking with an incredibly large number of people; third, fear is fear.

At its most basic level, fear is energy. It's sensation and information. That means that fear is not necessarily something to avoid; we can actually sit with and learn from it. Fear is just an uncomfortable anxious buzzing of the nervous system designed to impart information, to bring you back to attention and awareness, to reawaken your senses. The fear feeling is not so much about the object of fear—the thing we *think* we are scared of—but rather our perception and anticipation of an imagined negative outcome. The oft-quoted FDR line from his 1933 inaugural address pretty much nails it: "The only thing we have to fear is fear itself." Reading those words and believing them to be true is one thing; it's quite another thing to open more deeply to your own experience of fear, which is how you discover your courage.

\*

Not all speaking gigs are created equal. For me, one of the most coveted speaking experiences of all is a TED talk. So you can imagine my delight when I was accepted to speak at TEDx Santa Cruz in September of 2012. Okay, so it wasn't the "real" TED Conference, but it was a tremendous start. When I first found out, I felt elated, but then I started to get nervous. I was scheduled to speak to a sold-out crowd of over four hundred people at a gorgeous theater with flashy lights and multiple cameras; I was listed on the bill with several intimidatingly influential speakers I knew. Oh, and I would do it all with no notes or prompter.

I should mention that this wouldn't be my first rodeo behind the mic. I had taught in front of third and fourth graders for years, which *seemed* like excellent practice, and I had given dozens of poetry readings everywhere from dive bars to university classrooms across the country. However, there was one notable recent speech at the local Chamber of Commerce in which I broke out in a cold sweat, rambled incoherently about a new business I knew very little about, and felt it wise to describe the tingly sensations coursing through my bloodstream. That brave effort was met with puzzled looks, strained silence, and a few baffled snickers before I blushed beet red and made a dash for the door. In other words, I was *mostly* a seasoned pro. To prepare myself for speaking without notes in hand and with terror in my heart, I joined a Toastmasters group, practiced weekly, honed my skills by speaking at trade shows for work, and slowly improved.

However, as TEDx approached, I kept thinking about the production and the spectacle of it all, and my fears multiplied. *What if my voice gives out? What if they don't clap? What if I blank?* As the day of my talk got closer, the fear and anxiety gnawed further into the recesses of my ego, breaking it down. A nervous tinge turned into a stomachache, and then a chronic nauseous dread settled in. I scoured the web for speaking tips and principles on how to give a successful TED talk. I must have watched a million TED presentations in which I was overwhelmed by the inspiring ones and occasionally baffled by the average ones. I deepened my commitment to Toastmasters and when I compared myself to the newbies I felt pretty good about myself. But when I studied the speeches of Brene Brown and Elizabeth Gilbert I became filled with comparison-fueled terror—how could they appear so confident and natural, so relaxed and at ease with themselves? I rewrote my talk 427 times. I finally settled on something I thought was fairly decent and read it out loud in front of the mirror, to my dog, Jupiter, to the planet Jupiter and the rest of the night sky, to the framing canopy of trees in my yard. I read it over and over again until I was sick of it. I tried to embody my talk with gestures, imagining myself like Sir Richard Burton gearing up for *Macbeth* at the Royal Shakespeare Theatre. I was going to be *alive* on stage; I resolved to animate my body and speech and deliver something *profound*, dammit!

My memory has never been good. And I have never been particularly quick on my verbal feet—I'm not at my best ad-libbing or being spontaneous. Regardless of my effort, I feared this would spell certain doom. Although I committed the talk to memory, the day approached and my fear continued to chew away at my hopes of a flawless delivery.

I arrived at the theater filled with small bubbles of excitement that were drowned out by a leaden sea of dread. I met with the organizers, who told me casually to settle in. Then, with a cheery pat on the back, one of them said, "Oh, by the way, you'll be closing the whole event. No pressure! Ha, ha!" They chuckled. I gasped and sputtered, turned pale with fright, and tried not to vomit at their feet. "You'll do great," they assured me. I went back to the green room doubled over with terror. I tried to chitchat with the other speakers, but nothing came out of my mouth. I just paced around backstage, shaking and wringing my hands, sweating. I went for a walk around the building muttering to myself. I tried all my breathing exercises and meditation techniques. Nothing seemed to assuage the tight aluminum coils of fear vibrating in my stomach. I even got some bodywork done backstage, all to no effect. I was in over my head. I should bail, claim sudden illness, politely bow out. The day crept on agonizingly slow, closer and closer to my twelve minutes of shame. I had a hard time listening to the other speakers, let alone appreciating them.

And then there I was, being wired up and introduced. I practically ran out on stage, not so much excited as bewildered into motion, as if pushed into traffic. If I ran *at* the cars maybe they would swerve around me. But after a couple steps all I could muster was a limp jog. The cars revved their engines and sped toward me, headlights and shiny grills bearing down on me, eager faces waiting for me to regale them with profound insight, wisdom, and beauty packaged in a voice of startling authority and warmth. I began to speak. The words fell out of my mouth like small shards of broken glass. I was expecting to squeak, for my voice to crack and shutter, but what I heard instead was a terror-fueled mechanical propulsion coming through me from some distant galaxy. Regardless, I was on script, following along nicely. I kept a somewhat edgy pace, but I wasn't losing the thread. Between the stabs of abdominal pain, I even dared to consider that I might be on a roll. Until about ten minutes and forty seconds in, that is, precisely at the point when I was revving up for my big epiphany, the denouement, the zenith, my irresistible "call to action." I could almost hear the standing ovation.

And then I blanked. I stumbled over one of my lines, lost track of what came next, and went mute. I shouldn't say that I went *blank* exactly; there seemed to be a tangled pile of broken sentences somewhere far off in the foggy distance. And then I noticed the silence. It suddenly bore down on me with such intensity that I had to jump out of the way to avoid being crushed to death. I shrugged my shoulders and said conclusively, "I guess that's it." And then I ran off the stage. Rather, I slunk off, tail clenched between my legs, my entire body vibrating with grating humiliation. But I also felt a lazy puff of relief—I could at least crawl back into my invisible ego hole now and be done with the dread burning a hole in my stomach.

That was a few years ago. I still cringe when I think about blanking that night, but mostly I think of all the things I regret not doing. Mostly, I regret not connecting with the audience. As is often the case when speaking in large venues, I could barely see the people, which made me feel that they couldn't see me, so I just babbled away up there in my halo of invisibility. But I wasn't actually speaking to *them*—I was too busy managing my fear, trying to stay on my memorized script, and going through my rehearsed gestures. See, even though I was talking about vulnerable things, I wasn't actually *being* vulnerable. I put up this huge wall of perceived strength, memory, and togetherness, which crumbled because I wasn't actually feeling my experience. I was too busy trying to transcend the terror, trying to say the right thing, trying to be the star of the show. It was all about *me* when it should have been all about *them*. This is what great speakers (and writers) do—they make it about the audience. They connect with the audience, first and foremost. They don't get caught up being overly preoccupied with themselves—with how they're viewed, how much they're worshipped or loved, or anything else like that. Instead, they concern themselves entirely with *you*.

After all my years of teaching and speaking, I thought I understood this point. I mean, when I spoke to kids it was always about them, and I rarely got nervous. But in the lead-up to my TEDx talk, I exaggerated its meaning and invented a whole new level of importance to my presentation. I envisioned the ovation. I imagined it launching my career like it did for Brene Brown. So I carried on like a self-consumed madman. In spite of it all, I actually gave a decent talk—in terms of content, it might be one of the best talks I've ever given. It's just that my delivery was completely self-reflective, even self-absorbed, and that left little space for anyone else to hear it.

But I'm glad I did it. I learned more from that failure than any previous success I've had. Most importantly, I learned that I need to embody my truth not only in the process of writing but also in the process of speaking my written words aloud. As Theodore Roosevelt said (and Brene Brown further popularized), it's more honorable and preferable to fail "while daring greatly." For me, that means daring to be true to my words in writing and speaking.

But if you need further reminding of what *not* to do in a TEDx talk, go check out my presentation online. Then feel free to give me a standing ovation, from the comfort and safety of your own home.

> **TRY THIS**   Write down three things you can do in the next
> month that scare you. They don't have to be drastic acts such as
> speaking in front of four hundred people. How about just sitting
> down to write that first scene of your novel? Typing up your first
> few poems? That can be scary enough. And these frightening
> endeavors don't have to be related to writing. Maybe it's a little
> terrifying to sit in meditation with your eyes closed for more than
> five minutes. Check in with yourself and see what's a little scary
> for you—where can you push yourself a little further? Book a trip
> overseas, sign up for a rock-climbing adventure, agree to read at
> your local open mic. Keep in mind that you don't have to actually
> *do* these things right now. Simply start by writing them down and
> sitting in their presence for a bit. *Then* you can take action to feel
> your fear and do it anyway!

Audacity means allowing your desire to stand taller than your timidity, fear, and resistance. This holds true whether you're talking about writing, speaking, or anything. It's about stepping into a more powerful sense of self. Audacity in writing has to do with facing the emptiness of the page with full abandon and acknowledging your role in the world, realizing the importance of your particular contribution toward this great song of humanity, this epic tale humanity reflects back to the universe. Why should the insights, experiences, and reflections of Shakespeare (or insert your literary hero du jour here) be any more important than yours? They shouldn't be, and they're not!

I could have bailed on the TEDx talk. I could have bowed out. I could have let the terrifying sensations of fear and doubt hold me back. I could have seen the whole situation as a failure or as validation of my belief that I'm not a natural or talented speaker. Instead, I chose to *feel* the fear—the immense psychic and physical discomfort—and do it anyway. In fact, the very next thing I did after that TEDx event (well, after a couple months of recovery) was sign up for a speaker training, and then I enrolled in another. Years ago, when I was collecting rejection notice after rejection notice from countless literary journals (back when we sent actual letters with SASEs—self-addressed stamped envelopes), I would take the returned poems from one rejection letter and immediately insert them into a brand-new submission envelope for another journal. In other words, I would persevere.

I was recently listening to an interview with Brene Brown in which she talked about being genuinely vulnerable with an audience in advance of her famous TEDx talk. She wanted to be real, to simply reach out and connect by actually *being* vulnerable while *talking* about vulnerability. Her husband didn't think it was such a great idea, but she wanted to try it, at least once. So in this particular presentation, Brene spoke about her psychological breakdown, about being in therapy, about her fears and emotional slogs. After the talk, she felt terrible—she had really put herself out there. On the way home, she promised herself, "I will never do *that* again." She was mortified by what she had said and initially didn't want the organizers to post the speech. They did, and in the first month it was online, Brene's talk received over one million views. It's now been viewed more than twenty-five million times. Now, as Brene said on the *Tim Ferriss Show* podcast, "If I'm not a little bit nauseous when I'm done [with a talk], then I probably didn't show up the way I should have."

The blank page (as well as the empty cushion or chair) is your open stage, your field of possibility. This is your invitation to show up with courage and vulnerability. Your practice and process should feel a little uncomfortable, a little out of your cozy zone. Let audacity be your guide. Though you may not have an audience out there staring you down with expectation, you do have an audience *inside* who can be excruciatingly perfectionistic, self-critical, and self-doubting. When you meet the page with your vulnerable self, you transcend this critic with audacity.

Eventually your courage eclipses your fear. The more you can connect deeply with your raw emotional truth, with the actual experiences and emotional sensations—and then write from that vulnerable place—the more powerful, relatable, and effective your writing will be. It starts with mindful attention to those very emotions. Become intimate with your internal life and meet it head on with courage and trust. I know it doesn't always feel so smooth. Sometimes it feels like we're writing completely uninteresting, solipsistic purges, and at times that might be the case. But that's just a gateway. Be audacious, persevere, and keep on keepin' on! Doing so will reward you with insight, love, a strong heart, and the potential for great writing, as well as great compassionate being.

### → *Meditation on Audacity*

Let's begin with where we are—in a grounded and courageous place, fully embodied. Find your comfortable place to sit. Rest your hands easily in your lap and your feet flat on the ground or cushion. Gently close your eyes. Take a few breaths inward and release. Find that natural rhythm of your breathing, connecting with your breathing body. Tune into your immediate sensory experience, just noticing what your experience is right in this moment. Let your breath be your anchor and ground.

See if you can bring to mind a particularly scary or vulnerable situation. Think of one in which you recently felt exposed, vulnerable, even fearful; not one in which you were in a dangerous situation, but a memory of you putting yourself out there in some way—confronting someone, speaking to a group, asking someone new out on a date. As memories of the situation come to you, breathe deeply into your belly and know that you are safe now, breathing here in this moment in this body. If you need to, you can open your eyes, but try to remain grounded in your breathing body. Notice the rush of sensations and allow whatever arises to arise with love, patience, and compassion. Be gentle with yourself and remember that you are safe. See if you can stay with the feelings and simply explore how your fear or discomfort exists as bodily sensations. Notice where in your body you feel them. Breathe nurturing air into those places. Allow yourself to become familiar with the sensations of fear and vulnerability without the need to disconnect, distract, or avoid altogether. Be patient and kind with yourself as the emotions and feelings stream through. Gently note any physical changes: increased body heat, increased heart rate, tingling in your arms, increased sweating, and so on. Notice how the sensations linger, change, and dissipate. Become curious and open while kindly grounding yourself in the breath.

Put both hands on your heart, left on top of right, and take a deep breath. Say to yourself, "May I be well, may I be at peace, may I be bathed in the light of loving-kindness and compassion right now." Take another deep breath, exhale, and release your hands. Bring them back together, palm to palm, at your heart and bow to yourself in gratitude for your courage and love. Open your eyes to complete the meditation.

You might try this meditation for five minutes at first and then extend it as you feel more audacious and courageous. The more you allow the feelings to arise and exist, the more familiar you will become with them. In turn, you will become better able to let them go and dissipate and see them for what they are—waves of energy and information arising and passing away.

---

### Audacious Writing Exercise

Freewrite for ten minutes about something externally that scares you: certain people, public transportation, cars, airplanes, earthquakes, tsunamis, tornados, floods, fires—whatever. Be as honest as you possibly can. Remember that nobody has to see this, so feel free to be as ludicrous and irrational as you want to be. Write into your fear, specifically focusing on *how* and *where* you feel it in your body. How would you describe those sensations? What could you compare their movements to?

Now freewrite for ten minutes on an internal fear: loss of love, friendship, your own mind, physical abilities, etc. Perhaps it's a fear of loving too openly and having to let someone go, of being too joyous, of being ungrounded and living in a dream world.

# 8

# August
## {Devotion}

*Permission to Flow*

As we sink into the depths of summer—guided by the muse, buoyed by our audacity to take the creative-spiritual plunge, we deepen our commitment by being devoted. We are devoted not only to practice and process but also to self-inquiry; devoted not only to writing but also to the full exploration of our creative and spiritual potential.

Many years ago I served as a campground host at a remote state park cabin on a rugged section of the lost coast in Northern California. It was a time of wonderful solitude, creativity, and connection with the natural world. One evening around sunset I set off for a hike toward Chemise Mountain, a giant uplifted chunk of graywacke sandstone with a virtually sheer western face dropping a thousand feet straight down to the Pacific. On the way up I strolled through grassy meadows clumped with lavender iris and past a favorite weathered-to-bright-bone eucalyptus that refused to fall. Then I hiked along the volcanic sea walls of Whale Gulch and wove my way through a dappled forest of alders. Up and up I hiked along the narrow trail until I found myself at the top of that cliff edge a thousand feet above the ocean. The waves crashed far below. I felt them thrumming through my body with the muffled roar of thunder; I saw their tiny foam doilies shifting across the beach far below. I came around a soft bend in the trail and there facing me was a huge male tule elk with a rack of antlers like the majestic reach of an old-growth oak. Our eyes met. We stared each other down, frozen in time, suspended in the salt air in a kind of magical embrace, species to species. I'm not sure how long we stayed like that, but it felt like a brilliant sliver of eternity.

At that moment, my heart burst open, my senses amplified—I noticed the horizon line and how it halved the elk, how the evening light grazed his wet nose, and I smelled his musky scent. I stepped forth in a daze, my surroundings glowing as he unceremoniously wandered off into the brush. The ocean rushed my eyes and receded, the redwoods laughed, the clouds breathed in sync with my lungs, the alder leaves shimmered electric green and began to giggle. "Who need be afraid of the merge?" boomed Walt Whitman in *Leaves of Grass*, echoing in the air like an omniscient god. I looked around to see if anyone else heard it. There was no one else. And so, in that moment I surrendered to the whole weird magical brilliance of the experience—tears glistening at the corners of my eyes. At that moment, the self I knew as Albert merged into elk and alder, ocean and sky. I became awake to the immense presence and infinite beauty of this wild and mysterious world, and realized, yes, *I am that!*

*

We are what we do—what we are present to, what we are open to. We are our actions. Devotion is concentrated intentional action. Where our attention in mind goes, either by default or (hopefully) with bright awareness, our bodies follow in action. Devotion is about commitment, fealty, affection, ardor, and love, in no particular order. Devotion to self means making a vow to self, a vow to presence. What have you taken vows to or for, either consciously or unconsciously, in your life?

I could have spaced out and dismissed the above encounter with the elk. I mean, I'd seen dozens of them in the previous weeks. This time, however, I stayed put; I consciously took several deep breaths and devoted myself to this simple yet profound moment of merging with *what is*. This experience reminded me viscerally that there is no other spiritual moment—all moments are spiritual when we are awake. Which isn't to say we need to walk around as bug-eyed ecstatics every moment of our lives, but we can become more brightly and lovingly attuned to the divine presence found in the ordinary instants of every day through devotional, practiced attention—breath by breath.

Traditionally, *devotion* in religious-spiritual terms means surrendering to some separate god, a powerful (and sometimes terrifying) entity outside of yourself. In contrast, by *devotion* I'm referring to surrendering to that infinite creation energy and spiritual mystery that is you! This kind of devotion can take shape as a mystical experience while hiking on a coastal mountaintop or meeting the face of a stranger on the streets of New York City. The common factor is an open and awake you.

Devotion in spirituality at its most basic level means committing to presence; it means showing up with your full self at any given moment, with an open, patient, and compassionate heart—no matter the shadow of the judgmental mind, no matter the situation. Devotion in writing and creativity is no different. It starts in the immediacy of the personalized moment when you feel all of creation at your back, cheering you on toward a commitment to growth, creativity, and learning. And you meet that support by breathing into your full potential, by surrendering to an expanded evolution of the self.

To devote yourself to presence means to devote yourself to the infinite flow of divine creativity. It starts on the grand scale—the infinite universe—and then shows up personally as it manifests in your watercolor painting, sculpture, relationships (the ultimate works of art), poem, memoir, or novel. There are no blocks, no limits, because there is no separation. This is the truth of awakening. You writing your novel is your novel being written through a more open and free you. You writing your memoir is you writing the script of your life. And it begins with a vow to presence. Just be willing to show up and become more awake—moment to moment, breath by breath.

> **TRY THIS**    What does devotion mean to you? What does your
> devotion look like in action? Write down seven things you are
> devoted to in your life. Start with a simple list by just naming them.
> Then write a short narrative or poem about each one. Freewrite
> into the details of this person, place, or thing. What aspects are you
> specifically devoted to and why?

Now it's true that sometimes it can feel like there actually is a block, that there is a limit, to our creative or physical abilities, to our access to resources (financial or otherwise), to changing emotional reactions and patterns, or even to making certain relationship connections. Sure, but it's important to remember that limitation is mere perception, manufactured resistance based on outside conditioning—societal, familial, cultural—showing up as fear, doubt, jealousy, and so on. Remember that feelings are sensations, and sensations are simply energy and information. They come in bleats and pulsations and then disappear. Ever notice? They are transient, fleeting, temporary. Our goal is to not get overly caught up in the momentary, but align and remain devoted to *that which never ceases*—the background source of all emotion, all creativity itself. Another word for this is *emptiness*—the void that is our true nature.

We don't ever want to *deny* our emotions or push them away. Instead, we want to sit with them fully and feel deeply into them with all the associated grief and anguish, along with the rush of tears and complex energies of the body. Dissipating or releasing feelings we've held tightly in our body can take two days or two years or even twenty-two lifetimes, depending on our individual situation. Regardless, remain patient, seek support, and pace yourself. Feel the emotions as thoroughly as you can until they pass. Watch how they arise, live in you for a while, and then fade away. In particular, pay attention to your bodily experience as your feelings arise and fall. Ask yourself honestly and compassionately what benefit you get from identifying or associating with those sensations. Then consider that the infinite creative *you* is far larger than any passing emotion.

Devotion is not an act of convenience. Sadly, it's not about checking in with yourself in the morning to see how devoted you feel. Personally, I stopped asking a long time ago whether I felt like writing (I'd often rather be on my bicycle pedaling through the forest). The question isn't helpful. In true devotion, we don't succumb to the vagaries of our moods. That isn't to say that moods don't show up—you bet they do. Nor does it mean you don't deserve to take a break and chill on the couch with a bowl of popcorn every once in a while. Rather, if following your moods is your default avoidance tactic, you will notably limit your creative potential. Mother Teresa didn't wake up every morning in the shit-filled, disease-ridden, death-strewn streets of Calcutta and say, "Gee, I don't really feel like running my charity and feeding people today. I think I'll have a bag of chips and an orange soda and head to the mall!" Not that she didn't occasionally take a well-deserved break (though I doubt it included potato chips, orange soda, or the mall). She may even have experienced mood swings, not to mention, as her letters show, a major crisis of faith and, at times, a complete absence of God. But her vow to God and her devotion to the community were far stronger than the occasional fleeting sense of not feeling up to it all.

Your approach to the page every day as a devoted writer and your approach to the cushion as a devoted meditator are no different. Attitude is everything. Reminding yourself of your devotion to Self (with a capital *S*) is everything. Your shit-filled, disease-ridden, and death-strewn streets are the doubt-addled, procrastination-chewed corridors of your own heart and mind. You're familiar with the nagging voices of resistance, I'm sure—the ones that tell you it's already been done, that you can never write like so-and-so, that you suck, that you're too tired, too hangry, too lazy, too crazy, or too whatever. They don't quiet easily, so whenever you hear them, take a deep breath and say your prayers (whatever that means to you). Then remind yourself of your mission, commitment, and devotion. Go sit in silence, take a walk in the woods or through the park, stretch your body, or drink a latte—whatever it takes to get you back to yourself, and, in turn, back to the page.

Devotion goes beyond mere interest and soft curiosity, though it may start there. Let it blossom into habit, commitment, and mission. Let it start with compassion for the self and then grow into compassion for those around you. Eventually there is a tipping point at which you realize you can't *not* do this writing thing. It becomes an obsessive mission. At this point, you have become devoted to the path of writing, to the journey of awakening.

\*

Talented people are nothing if not devoted. Here's a useful equation:

$$devotion + attention + consistent\ action = TALENT$$

Basically you love something (for example, writing, volleyball, mothering) so much that you not only want to consume it but you also want to contribute to the further expression and evolution of that thing. This is a democratic definition of talent that says anyone with enough interest, enthusiasm, and devotion can jump in at any time and play. It's up to you to decide at what level you want to engage. Your success is directly proportionate to your level of devotion, practice, consistency, and persistence. Successful figure skaters, mountain bikers, singers, painters, and writers all have a different relationship with practice, and that relationship is based on devotion. Here's the secret: they're not always in the mood. Even so, they hit the ice, the trail, the studio, the canvas, and the page anyway. When they feel sore, tired, upset, doubtful, fearful, groggy, frustrated, angry, torn, stymied, baffled, and broken, they do what they need to do. They practice when they have a cold, when their work is stressful, when their mom is in town, when the temperature plummets or rises, and when the mortgage is overdue. You get the point. There's nothing particularly magical about it.

What role will writing or meditation play in your life? At what level do you want to play? You get to choose. The devotional part of talent is about surrender, affinity, and generosity. Who do you want to *become* through this practice? How do you want to serve the greater good? At a certain point you realize this isn't about you—that tiny egoic voice clanging around in your head. It's about *them*—your family, your community, the larger society. It's about a bigger, shared vision for connection and wholeness. The practice becomes the prayer, your vehicle of service. That's when you go from distractible yearning and confused scribbler to determined, focused, generous, and mindful writer. At this point, you'll find the wind at your back. *Upepo* they call it in Swahili. Some Native Americans refer to the Spirit Wind or the Great Spirit. Christians speak of the grace of God and Buddhists use terms such as *Buddha nature* or *shunyata*. You might have heard *Source Energy* mentioned in New Age/New Thought circles. Whatever the term, now is your time to tap into the sacred creation energy that emanates from within you, ushering you along the path of awakening to your true creativity.

*

Asking how you can become a writer, or a great writer, isn't a helpful question. It's kind of like asking how you can become an awakened, enlightened being. You can't become what you already are. In Western culture, we think we have to accumulate more knowledge, more insight, more experience. We believe if we hang out with famous teachers we'll become enlightened, and if we study with celebrated writers we'll become like them, too. This type of thinking also isn't helpful. Instead, we need to realize that *we* already possess all the answers and gifts we'll ever need. This isn't to say that it's not useful to learn from spiritual teachers or attend readings and retreats with writers. Of course—all that can be quite important. But true learning only comes from within *you* via your own integration, assimilation, and letting go.

You might ask yourself a more reasonable question like, "How do I get *better*?" or "How do I *improve*?" When I talk about meditation, I regularly hear people say things like, "Oh, I could never do that" or "I'm a terrible meditator." To me, that's silly—we're talking about sitting and breathing. In other words, we're talking about something available to all of us, and it's not something we can equate with quality or proficiency. I think what most people mean when they talk about their troubles with meditation is that they want to quiet their chattering mind and settle their squirming body. Me, too!

Part of the answer is literally in your hands. It's why I wrote this book. In terms of devotion, start by experimenting with the practices herein and see what changes they bring to your writing and meditation practice, and, in turn, your life.

When we're talking about writing, the question of "getting better" seems more reasonable. After all, there are good writers and bad writers, right? Clearly, some people can weave smooth, connective, dynamic sentences and some can't. And I suppose we can also say that there are conscious people and unconscious people, or wise and unwise people. In the relative sense, yes—all true. But for the moment let's not get caught up in the relative world. Instead, let's focus where true transformation occurs—on the internal-spiritual level.

Simply put, a writer is someone who writes. A Buddha is someone who is awake, who wakes up to that truth. If you call yourself a writer, and if you act and behave like a writer, you will soon *be* a writer. Likewise, an awakened being is someone devoted to presence, to source, to spirit. They don't just read or think about it—they practice in order to dwell within presence itself. As the distinguished meditation teacher Sylvia Boorstein suggests in the title of her book, "Don't just do something, sit there!" (And devotedly, I might add.)

By and large, spiritually awake people don't see themselves as separate from the discipline of spirituality. Similarly, accomplished writers don't see the practice of writing as something separate from their lives. It *is* their lives. They *live* their writing even when they aren't sitting down scribbling or typing away. They aren't moving toward a preferred state of mind and away from what's present in the moment. And yet too many of us wait for a spontaneous behavioral shift to make it all happen. Or we hope for some rare illuminating insight, thinking that external circumstance will knock us into awakening or into actualizing our dreams of being a writer. The moment to realize is always now! So stop thinking about it, pick up the pen, and *be* that devotional spark in this very moment!

*

Because I love this sentence so much, I'm going to write it again: *practice doesn't make perfect, practice makes process, and eventually, with consistent attention, proficiency.* I'll also add: *and with serious devotion, mastery.* Now there's a loaded term—*mastery.* It just reeks of dominance and exclusivity, doesn't it? If it could, *mastery* would place itself in the upper echelon of the dictionary, the top 1 percent of words, right up there with *grandiloquent.* But it's true in writing and meditation: *practice doesn't make perfect, practice makes process, and eventually, with consistent attention, proficiency, and with serious devotion, mastery.* Most people give up before they engage in a habitual and meaningful process, but you can't have proficiency without process. And you can't even get close to mastery without devotion.

When they gave Ted Berrigan his master of arts degree, he gave it back, famously saying, "I am the master of no art." Hilarious, and true. Just because you have a degree from an accredited institution doesn't mean you have fully mastered the craft. Believe me—I have a master of fine arts degree in something called "new genres," whatever that means. In addition to the fact that those new genres are probably now considered old, I certainly never mastered the visual fine arts—far from it. Sadly, the statistics on how many people are still writing or making art five years after receiving their degrees are rather dismal. The difference between Berrigan and most of his graduate-school peers is that Ted continued to practice—he developed a process that became habitual, even obsessive. In turn, he became proficient and—in the eyes of many—a master.

Ever notice how elite athletes are devoted to their game? Their devotion is usually rooted in the love of play, exploration, and discovery. Their practice becomes their path to awakening. Having gained proficiency and even mastery through devotion results in humility, patience, compassion, and love. Yes, it's challenging—even grueling. But incredible joy, freedom, and accomplishment await you on the other side.

### ➜ *Devotion Meditation*

To enter this devotion meditation, let's begin again with our introductory instructions:

Close your eyes and take a deep breath. Exhale slowly. Take a second deep breath and exhale, and then a third. Let your breath be natural and let your body rest at ease. Breathe into any areas of tension and let them release and relax a little with each breath. What does it feel like to be embodied in this moment? Breathe in, breathe out. You have absolutely nowhere to go and nothing else to do other than sit here and breathe. You are in a state of sincere perfection in this moment with nothing to add or take away, nothing to learn or acquire. There is nothing you need to fix, change, or manipulate in this moment. You are allowed to let everything be as it is. Breathe in and breathe out, letting go into the vast accepting beauty of this moment, whatever arises, holding this self with love and compassion.

In this moment, what comes to mind when I ask you, what are you truly devoted to? Think of it in terms of your life's purpose—what does that look like for you? What is your reason for being? What fills you with excitement, positivity, and love? Where does your devotion lie in this time? Take a deep breath and then exhale. Breathe into your deeply felt sense of devotion. Is it for family, community, creativity, or presence? Is it for healing, balance, abundance, or belonging? Breathe into the truth of whatever arises for you in this moment. Open your eyes or ring a bell to complete the meditation.

---

### ➜ *Devotion Writing Exercise*

Grab your notebook and freewrite on your purpose for ten minutes. What is your reason for being? What are you devoted to in this lifetime? Just allow the words to spill out and through you. Don't worry about spelling, grammar, punctuation, or any kind of correctness. Let whatever wants to arise come out and find freedom on the page. There is no right or wrong, no *should* or *should not*, no proper or improper purpose. Just try to touch into what's true for you in this moment.

# Autumn

# 9

# September
## {Revelation}

*The Essence of Story:*
*A Journey to the Center of the Self*

S eptember. The sun sinks lower, the days begin to get shorter and cooler, the heat and punch of summer wanes—change and transformation are afoot. After the slow cook of summer—after we have had our fun and have been stirred into our audacity, after we have become emboldened with the muse and have aroused our devotion—everything now aches to be revealed through our stories of change.

According to the dictionary app on my iPhone (that final cultural authority not to be questioned), the first antonym listed for *story* is *truth*. I find that interesting since we often associate the word *story* with fabrication and invention, if not outright lies. Which makes sense, right? Fable, fiction, tall tales . . . all these come from invention. Yet the origins of the word *story* point to the telling or writing down of events, as an account of things that actually happened—in other words, the "facts." There's more: my dictionary app also includes in the definition of *story* "relation of incidents," and then—in parentheses—"true or false." Of course, *story* can also refer to the "floor of a building." One explanation for this is that in the Middle Ages the fronts of buildings were sometimes decorated with rows of painted windows that narrated particular events. Hence, the terms *first story*, *second story*, *third story*, and so on. I don't have any profound point to make here, except to note some fun contradictions in our understanding of the word *story*. Stories are both true *and* false, fact *and* fiction. Either-or reasoning and other forms of black-and-white thinking don't apply to stories, which necessitate a both-and frame of mind. If you think about it, even the most wacky and absurd fantastical tales have some modicum of truth (if only symbolically) at their core. "Fiction is the lie through which we tell the truth," said philosopher and writer Albert Camus.

*

The various stories of our lives live within us in innumerable ways. You've heard the sarcastic or cynical comment, "Oh, my god—it's the story of my life!" said when something unfortunate or repeatedly frustrating happens. "The story of my life" could also refer to a period when we came of age dramatically—a week of shocking joy or horror, or a fleeting transformative moment. Certain events get embedded in our consciousness and tend to shape not only our daily behavior but also the entire course of our life. Story is the very essence of who we are. It's how we define ourselves—these intricate tales that pattern our consciousness with repetition.

But the stories we tell ourselves *about* ourselves are certainly not fixed. We constantly move them around, reinvent and re-create them. We don't have to be limited by these events—these perceived facts of our lives—nor an inherited or conditioned sense of ourselves as beings created by these stories. Stories take place around us all the time. Part of waking up requires tuning in and becoming more aware of the stories we tell ourselves, as well as the infinite array of stories playing out around us all the time. They have a lot to teach us about reality, truth, beauty, our own creativity, and the potential for transformation.

*

It's a rare rainy day in early September. I'm sitting in a slick new café on Fourth Street, peering out from my favorite table in the corner.

The boisterous barista just said, "Effort is what life's made of," to some bearded, hunched-over hipster in a black hoodie carrying a blue skateboard. She's working hard but somehow effortlessly. She sports a black-and-white floral blouse, black jeans, black shoes, and a black-clip lip ring that miraculously keeps her lisp-free. She authentically and generously quips and banters with whoever appears before her. She is not faking it, not doing it for the boss. She is sage. Tom Waits helps her through the shift, belching on the Victrola. I laugh out loud for calling it a *Victrola*. My computer just put a red line under it; it doesn't even recognize it as a word. My mother would have said such a thing (Hi, Mom! What are you doing here?)—she referred to any electronic device that emitted sound as a Victrola, even though a Victrola was a brand of gramophone record player from the 1940s, just like Kleenex is a brand of tissue.

Mom never figured out how to use a cell phone. Before she died she once asked me to call her on the Victrola. That's not actually true. I totally made that detail up in the midst of my freewrite, thinking it would add something to my anecdote. It's fun to invent things as a writer, to embellish stories. This is a natural human urge—perhaps a survival mechanism or primal need. It's tempting to have invention take precedence over reality. R-E-A-L-I-T-Y, whatever that is.

Back to my freewrite: The assignment I was following said to write about what's in front of me, so here we are. My REI Nalgene water bottle is in front of me, taking center stage, as the baristas strut in the background, like emo flamenco dancers. How about some similes? Books burst blurry in the distance like a field of wildflowers as I polish off my mocha latte and a narrow slice of almond blueberry cake (perfectly delicious BTW). My water bottle is filled with water, lime juice, and cranberry. I am so in love with cranberry juice. It's weird, really, just how much I appreciate cranberry juice for its caustic tart snap, its hidden sweetness. Its mere existence makes my life so much more joyous.

Peppy barista with pierced lip. That's a much better sentence. Tom Waits still belches against clash of dishes being smashed around in gray plastic bus tub. Whoosh of tires spinning down rain-slick belly of Fourth Street every time someone swings open the door as a cold, wet breeze blasts forth behind them. Our barista greets every new arrival with the same sense of excitement and enthusiasm as if greeting her parents' best friends—scratch that, her own best friends, friends she hasn't seen in weeks. Their less-than-enthusiastic responses don't seem to faze her. "Give me an Americano," barks one grumpy dude, avoiding eye contact. Barista responds, "Don't worry, sir, our lovely barista Sarah will have that caffeine flowing through your veins in no time." She smiles at him, tilting her head and winking. He turns away but cracks an uncomfortable grin. Most who show up here get knocked out of their self-absorbed stupors by the barista's brightness. I know I am.

What if you were like that with everyone you met? Would it be exhausting for you, annoying to them? Would they be enchanted, offended, nonplussed, merely uplifted, or permanently transformed? It's amazing how much authentic, enthusiastic presence can change us. Snap us back into gratitude. A woman with a newborn just came in looking exhausted and forlorn. Barista starts cooing and saying how beautiful her baby looks. "How can I help you, sweetheart?" I thought the woman was going to cry. I almost did. No one has called her sweetheart in weeks, possibly ever, certainly not her boyfriend, who has all but bailed on her and the kid. This woman appeared on the verge of a meltdown, overwhelmed with her burden of being a single mom, sleep deprived, her asshole boyfriend not showing up yet again. She didn't get the raise at work she was hoping for, and to top it off, she just got a parking ticket.

I made most of that up. Call it projection, fiction, white lies, bending the truth, or hyperbolizing a simple encounter. You get the idea. See how we do this? It could be art making at its best, or illusion making at its worst. Practice knowing the difference.

Back in my little fib, the baby is fussing. And our heroine-barista shows up like a magical auntie with full presence, full engagement, and even love for this complete stranger. What must we know to love? Can we be our authentic, enthusiastic self no matter what and show up for each other? Maybe you are at work and you have to perform some customer service schtick to keep your job, but you do it not because it's your job and you want to please your boss (or merely keep the job); you do it because *this is the most important moment of your life*—the only moment of your life. You don't know what's going to happen next. Here in reality, all we have is now. Your work—regardless of your actual *job*—is to meet the world head on, at this very moment, no matter what, no matter who. Meet whatever grief, trauma, fear, anxiety, or illusion that shows up with as much joy, presence, and enthusiastic aliveness as you can muster. Say *yes* to whatever comes.

And that is freewriting. That is free being, free living, and free storytelling on the path to awakening.

## TYPES OF STORY

Story shows up in our experience in two primary ways. First, the personal "story of our lives"—the collective experiences, memories, people, family, and so on. And second, there are the stories we create as writers crafting a novel, a play, a script, a poem sequence, even a memoir—in other words, our written inventions.

And yet we also invent and reinvent ourselves all the time in "real life." On one hand, we've got the facts of our life and what we understand about the events we've experienced. I'm referring to the story we tell ourselves about ourselves, the story that is imprinted upon us by conditioning, memories, our parents, teachers, friends, and peers. This story includes our moral code, our likes and dislikes, our style and personality, our physicality and looks, and our sense of what we think is possible for ourselves in this lifetime. This story also contains all our hidden shames, doubts, fears, and failures, as well as our hopes, dreams, and aspirations.

On the other hand, we have the story we present to the world. This is our façade. It's a surface presentation we create based on how we wish the outside world to perceive us. This includes how we show up in certain relationships, the act we put on at work, even the role we play as a parent. We all do this to some extent—mostly it's called "getting through life"—and yet if we get lost in these façades, they can become hurtful. In extreme examples, this can show up as chronic lying, delusional behaviors, or bipolar and dissociative disorders.

Sometimes we get caught up in our own creations and we overidentify with a particular role or personality. We want others to view us as unique and interesting, so we construct a certain persona—and sometimes it's to the detriment of our well-being. When the story of ourselves becomes limiting and seemingly fixed, it can stunt our further growth and personal evolution. We need to remember that these identities are never fixed—they are not our true self. They are like costumes we put on for a time and then discard when the party—that phase of life, that relationship, and, eventually, life itself—is over.

There lies within us always the potential for change and reinvention. Perhaps you've experienced a devastating loss or a difficult childhood filled with challenging relationships. Maybe you are burdened with financial difficulty or career roadblocks. Regardless, you can always create a new story of possibility for yourself. We are always the sum total of how and what we think of ourselves—the stories we tell ourselves about ourselves.

Brief example: I was struggling along as a marginally published poet, teaching poetry in the schools, making barely enough money to live on, when I was "interrupted" by the need to make a more substantial living. My wife, who was a social worker and burned out on her psychotherapy practice, came up with the idea of starting a homecare business. Neither of us had any business experience, and I certainly didn't have any health, homecare, or social work experience. Nor was I sure I wanted to take on a major business start-up project. After all, I was a writer. "Why can't I just make a decent living as a writer and teacher?" I complained to the universe. I reluctantly gave my blessings to my wife for this project and told her I would help with marketing and promotion. Next thing I knew we were buying into a franchise homecare agency—together—basically betting everything we had on a business that neither of us had much experience with.

It was time for me to change my tune, my story. I went from an old story of struggling, financially strapped, poet-teacher guy to a new story of homecare business owner guy. I had to learn and then embody a whole new persona and language for this business endeavor. It felt awkward and uncomfortable at first. I kicked and screamed and rebelled. It felt alien. I felt like a fraud. Fortunately, the entire business model was based on helping families find quality care for their aging parents, which I could certainly get my head around. I like to think of myself as a nice guy who likes to help people. What I had a harder time accepting was the possibility that I would have to abandon my writing career (which was mostly a possibility I created in my head).

Turns out I had learned a few business skills (which are really people skills) while teaching kids and "selling" our poetry program to school principals and parent-teacher organizations. Even so, I didn't feel like a business guy. So I started dressing the part: I went from jeans and sweaters to Brooks Brothers button-downs and gray flannel slacks. I had to wear a badge and attend senior care networking meetings, chamber mixers, and business luncheons, all of which made me squirm. It felt like a dramatic fake character makeover. I didn't write for months while we built the business from the ground up, and I spent all my time doing exciting things like attending PowerPoint presentations on the ins and outs of the homecare industry. It was challenging, but I pressed on.

Eventually, I missed writing too much; I had to get back to it. I wrote on the weekends, at five in the morning, at my lunch hour—whenever I could find a spare minute or two. And we eventually hired some help in the office, which allowed me to take a week off to go to Lake Tahoe to write.

Our business grew. And as we became more successful, I was able to pull away more, but I was changed. I now possessed new skills, new insights, and a new sense of possibility. After seven years of growing our business, my public speaking ability improved, my people skills expanded, and my sense of compassion deepened from visiting with the chronically ill and dying. I never gave up on my meditation and writing practices, I simply reworked them into a new schedule and new context. Although that time in my life seemed less than ideal for my writing career, it was during that time that I wrote and published a memoir and my first novel.

**TRY THIS**   Identify at least three ways in which you are caught up in the "story of your life"—any habit or pattern that habitually limits your career, relationships, spirituality, finances, or community. Think about ways in which you feel trapped in your personality or even held captive by your past. Call to mind certain dramatic situations and challenges. What stories do you tell yourself about these situations? Can you let go of some of these stories and their grip on your current (and, in turn, future) experience? Spend some time freewriting into the details of these stories.

## WRITING AND REWRITING THE STORY OF OUR LIVES

What are your deepest aspirations and goals, your daily intentions? Take a moment today to write them down—it helps to get clear and precise about what you want. I knew that I wanted to make money to support my family while offering something of value to the community, but I also wanted to stay connected to my creativity. It helped me tremendously to have a written reminder during that time, something I could refer to when I became overly busy or distracted. So what do you want in your life? Write it down and make those ideas something more than mere wishes—make them come alive in your experience. Maybe you want more financial security, or maybe you yearn to travel to Iceland or Argentina. Maybe you want to keep in better touch with your friends, or maybe your thing is exercising at least three times a week. Whatever it is, write it all down. Setting an intention (putting it on paper) and applying mindfulness to your goals will make them far more likely to happen. Remember when I said that writing is one of the most powerful points of focus we have as human beings? This is why. Through writing we generate the power to manifest our dreams. We can even create miracles.

**TRY THIS**   Go ahead and take time right now to answer the questions above and write down at least six specific goals for your life in the next year. Include the following areas: Spirituality,

Creativity, Health/Fitness and Wellness, Relationship, Financial/Job/Business, Community. Be specific about what you want in each area. Give yourself a time frame. Be realistic and honest with yourself. Push yourself, but don't set yourself up for failure. Connect with others to keep the dream alive and be held accountable. (Check out the events page on my website for wonderful ways to engage with a supportive community that can help make your writing and living dreams a reality!)

Some things to remember when you're writing to re-create your personal story: When you're working toward your dreams, you'll inevitably feel doubt, frustration, and fear. That's natural. It's extremely important to never deny those emotions. Feel them fully. Stay as present as possible to them, feel their full impact, and then let go. Instead of dwelling on how far you have to go (and how much it hurts to not be where you want to be in life right now), turn your attention to appreciating and feeling positive for what you currently *do* have. Return to the brighter intentions for your life in relationships, financial matters, career, creativity, or spirituality again and again. If you ground yourself in the positivity and beauty of your aspirations, you will begin to shine brighter day by day. Write out those dreams and aspirations repeatedly, as they change and evolve, and you will move closer to them. This is *not* passive journaling in which you place blame and complain about your troubles. Although doing that from time to time might feel nice and can work as a sort of release, I recommend that you focus your writing on what is working in your life, what you are truly grateful for. Write these feelings down with vigor and enthusiasm, and revisit the goals by reciting them daily.

## Drama in Writing Story versus Drama in Living Life

I want to go over classic story structure to see how it can apply to your creative writing practice in regards to novels but also to your real-life story. The key difference here: When you invent a creative story, you are seeking to *heighten* the drama, conflict, tension, and stakes. However, in your own life, you are seeking to *lessen* all of that. That might seem obvious, but sometimes we create drama in our lives without being totally conscious of doing so. It's not that we can totally avoid conflict and drama in our lives, but with practiced mindfulness we can reduce the amount of high drama—addictions, job loss, turmoil in relationships, emotional and health challenges, and so on. Mindfulness and deep awareness also help us to decrease our reactivity to the inevitable difficulties that arise in life. That is, we become better able to work through our challenges with compassion, insight, and trust. In other words, we don't see life as much through the lens of problems to be solved but rather as situations to be worked through for growth.

Here's a personal example: When my mother was dying, I felt extremely sad. I grieved, I cried, I prayed. Old issues came up in my awareness and then dissolved. I went to my mother and told her what she meant to me, how much I loved her. I did this with no expectations of reciprocation beyond what I knew she was capable of in the moment. I made a conscious decision to sit with the tough emotional memories; I chose to experience the sadness and grief and let it wash through me. I discovered that *being with* these feelings was actually cleansing. In my experience, it's the resistance that's hard. We often feel inclined to resist or deny such intense feelings, but in my experience this tendency just causes us more trouble. I decided to allow it all. I felt overpowered for a few days, but after that I felt enlivened, even opened up and relieved in a way. The extent to which I opened myself to the grief was the extent to which beauty, love, new insight, and possibility offered themselves to me. I decided I didn't need to get caught up in seeing her death only as a tragedy. I chose not to see myself as a victim of her death—that is, I didn't translate the feelings of loss as some problem that shouldn't be happening to me. Yes, my mom died too early. Yes, she died without much warning. And yet death is one of the fundamental truths of human existence. As the saying goes, "Argue with truth (reality) and you lose every time."

Around this time, my friend Carol and her sister were also dealing with the loss of their mother. Their situation was not unlike my own; unfortunately, they also experienced a lot of alcoholism, abuse, and neglect in their household. A lot of complicated emotional issues were tied up in their relationships with their mother, and though I can't speak for the dynamics of their situation, I want to note some differences in our responses to a similar loss. Keeping in mind that the relationship between mothers and daughters is quite different from the one between mothers and sons, I witnessed Carol and her sister experiencing their mother's death as largely devastating and tragic. They felt snowed by unresolved longings, frustrations, and feelings of abandonment. For them, their mother's death was a *problem*. Their responses were fairly extreme—one completely checked out and left the country, not even showing up for the funeral. The other didn't eat much of anything for weeks, broke out in shingles, and fell into depression.

During times of emotional distress, it seems as if we have no control, that we have no other options, that our sensations are things just happening *to* us. I'm not here to make a judgment about responses to various dramatic life-altering events, other than to say that in my experience we have more choice in any given moment than we think. Radical change *is* possible. Choosing a new story of strength, resilience, and empowerment is your birthright. What are you going to choose? When the inevitable dramas arise, which they will, can you remain a little more present and be with the accompanying cascade of feelings? Or will you deny and reject, trying to escape the emotional onslaught with alcohol, sleeping pills, reckless sex, or food? I encourage you to choose consciousness. Choose surrender and vulnerability. Seek out professional support that helps you connect with your inner resources in order to build up the courage to endure the grief. And reconnect with the divine source—it will catch you when you fall, hold you, and remind you of your own deep strength.

What does all this have to do with writing and story? I'm so glad you asked. Telling your story is a participatory act. It's an act of courage. It means choosing to engage the conversation of your life with insight, perspective, and a little distance. Doing so will allow you to see the archetypes, patterns, and underlying human struggles for redemption. So, back to you *writing* your story. Make sure you're familiar with the following components to give your writing the depth, breadth, and attention it deserves. As you're working on your own story, freewrite on the following questions to create the basic building blocks of what you long to say:

1. **Setting, situation, and initiating incident.** Where are we? What sets your story in motion? Who is leading us in? Ideally, your beginning should be a dynamic, somewhat mysterious, quirky, or strange place. Or at least profoundly ordinary. We should encounter something funny, batty, or alarming right from the beginning. Drop us into an edgy and new experience.

2. **Plot.** What happens, and how? Why do events happen? What are the key situations, actions, and primary events in your story that are critical to your hero's motion forward? What are the steps in his or her evolution?

3. **Characters.** What makes a person interesting? What makes a character dynamic? Think about the most memorable people in your life—maybe they're baffling, annoying, contradictory, opinionated, or just plain quirky. Maybe their desires and obsessions get in the way of their hopes and dreams. How do they act in response to their addictions, denials, and guilts? How do they respond to adversity? What are their habits, annoying tics, or funky mannerisms? Who do they bump up against, and why? To put it profoundly, what triggers their shit? Show us their reactivity, their weakness, their dark side. Every cast member should exist in your story for a reason, either contributing to your hero's evolution or creating a barrier to it.

4. **Scenes.** At the heart of inspiring drama, you'll find specific scenes of emotional revelation. You'll find brightness and juxtaposition. Show your readers where your character is going and where they've come from. Note their points of evolution along the

way. How can you make your scenes as vivid as possible? What striking details or symbols do they include? Be sure to include compelling backdrops and punchy dialogue.

5. **Conflict and opposition.** Nothing in life comes easy. Our plans get derailed by obstacles we never saw coming. What threatens your hero? Who stands in their way? How can you ratchet up the tension and make the action stand out? Make sure your hero enters into battle with a foe (literal or metaphoric) and comes out the other side either defeated or transcendent.

6. **Climax.** The battle eventually comes to a head. Your hero makes a life-changing decision, either forcibly by external situations and characters or by their own internal need. How does your hero get cornered? Why must they take action or die? What if they don't make it?

7. **Final resolution and ending.** What are we left with as readers? Relief? Uncertainty? A beautiful and sad surprise? A cliffhanger for the next installment? An unexpected twist? Perhaps a profound spiritual revelation? Make your ending memorable or poignant.

### → *Story Meditation*

Start by entering into the immediate momentary story of your body. Relax into your experience of your breathing body with eyes closed, feet flat on the ground, and hands at rest in your lap. Breathe in, breathe out. What are you experiencing in this very moment? See if you can be with simply what is. Tune into your sensory experience, breath by breath.

Now take a moment to bring to mind your story—the story of the person sitting here breathing. Who are you, really? Are you this temporary conglomeration of elements, this body of energy and information that will grow old and die? Are you the thoughts and ideas about yourself—a named, constructed self reimagined over and over again in your head? And where does this person go at night? Where was this person before your birth? Can you find this person somewhere inside your body?

Bring to mind your past. Let the images unfold as if in a movie, beginning with memories from early childhood, continuing on through your teenage years and young adulthood, and concluding with highlights that have brought you to this point in your life. This is the story of your life. Where are these memories now? Where do they exist? Take a deep breath and let the images go. How do you see the story of your life? How are the events arranged? See if you can detect any strong messages about limitations—what you can't do or who you can't be. What is possible and not possible in your life? Perhaps some of your memories are painful or sad. If so, extend love and kindness to yourself and allow those difficult feelings to flow through you. Take a deep breath and exhale. Place both hands on your heart, right hand on top of left. Repeat the following phrase silently to yourself or out loud: "I am not my story. I am a field of possibility." Take another deep breath and exhale. Say it again: "I am not my story. I am a field of possibility." Breathe in deeply again, breathe out, and for the third time: "I am not my story. I am a field of possibility." Open your arms wide as if to welcome in a new paradigm—a fresh and original story of possibility. Inhale deeply again, exhale, and open your eyes to complete the meditation.

---

### → Story Writing Exercise

Write a recent anecdote about something that happened to you or that you witnessed happening to someone else. Choose an event with some level of conflict or drama—a fight with your spouse, an argument with a cashier, a big move, a medical diagnosis, or the breakup of a relationship. Remember, you don't have to show this to anyone. Feel free to keep it safely locked in your journal.

You could also choose instead to freewrite on the outline of your life up to now (or a particular period of your life). This exercise will help you quite a bit if you plan to write a memoir or novel based on your life. Robin Romm's terrific memoir *The Mercy Papers* takes on the last three weeks of her mother's life. For my own memoir, *Beamish Boy*, I chose the three decades between ages seven and thirty-seven. You can write your own as messily as you wish. Just come up with a basic sense of story structure, your hero's journey, and how it applies to your own story (either fictionalized or real).

Write for at least thirty minutes and preferably an hour or longer. Start by simply telling us what happened, freewriting on the who, what, when, where, and how. Go back and reread; then plug in the following elements with the details from your own experience or imagination:

1. **Primary characters.** Tell us in more detail about the characters. Who is central to this story? What do your characters want? What do they crave or dream about? What do they avoid or obsess about? Describe something unique about them that doesn't have to do with their appearance—name a funny habit or mannerism.

2. **Setting.** Where does your story take place? Describe the smells, sounds, and tastes. Describe the colors, the mood in the air. What do you notice? Get specific. Name some objects in the room or in the background. Is anything off or out of place? Tell us all about the movement and action. If your setting were an animal, what would it say and do?

3. **Challenges and obstacles.** What prevents your characters from achieving their goals? Who stands in their way? What sets them off on their journey of discovery? Are they chasing an elusive dream or running away from a nightmare?

4. **Secondary characters.** Who are your main character's guides, allies, and mentors? Who are their antagonists or enemies? Give them names, describe them, and write them into your story. Show us in detail how they support or thwart your hero.

5. **Climax.** How does your hero overcome (or fail to overcome) their challenges? Is there a showdown with an enemy? What is your character's "do or die" moment? Tell us who else is involved, who has a stake in your main character's success or failure.

6. **Consequence, redemption, resurrection, and return.** Show us the evolutionary change in your hero. What have they given up or given in to? What (or who) did they have to leave behind? How have they grown and evolved? Is there a final twist or revelation to your story?

# 10

# October

## {Abundance}

### *The Five Senses and the Embodied Self*

We've done a lot over these past nine months. We've sown the seeds of becoming by immersing ourselves in reading. We've emerged from the snow-drunk dark of winter by cultivating our imagination through poetry. We've celebrated the lackadaisical heat of summer in song, amusement, and laughter. We've affirmed our courage and reestablished our devotion. Now it's time to celebrate the fruits of our labor by being fully awake and embodied to our experience. In other words, it's harvest time.

A transcendent sentence or line of poetry can make your mouth water or your stomach queasy. It can tighten your throat, hunch up your shoulders, and (my favorite) make your skin crawl. Great writing can give your nose an actual scent of disgust or make a scarlet-threaded memory tingle in your head like capillaries bleating beneath the skin. It can take you back in time to old, faded clips of a lonely snowy morning waiting at the bus stop, age eight, shivering under an elm tree. Writing can transmit goose bumps, chills, or even hives.

Writing into and from the body is about eliciting physical sensations from one body to the next via the magic of language. It's an act of engaging in a conscious, participatory stirring of emotional physicality—hand to head to heart to page. What we're aiming for is what Mary Karr refers to in *The Art of Memoir* as "sacred carnality," or what I like to call *enlightened viscerality*. Writing from the body means tuning into your sensory experience, feeling into your emotional experience, and reporting back to yourself with new insight and revelation. As they say, action speaks louder than words, but choice words strung together well upon the page can create physiological actions and reactions in the reader. And yet words also act as slick and slithery carriers of information, open to a variety of interpretations and experiences. The process of mindful writing invites you to reflect on these ideas; it asks you to reach deep within to access a wilder, more raw, and elemental self.

I'm talking about opening to a primordial self—a self of high rocky mountain passes, thin crisp air, churning rivers, beautifully tempestuous moody seas, and the scorching sun. Writing from the body is as messy and chaotic as nature herself—terrifyingly unpredictable and breathlessly delicate in a brilliant tangle of simultaneity. Writing from the body is an emotionally engaged heart-to-heart with the elemental you and your immediate contact with the rough beauty of the world. Naked body flat upon cool river stones, you write with sun rays in hand, water droplets at your fingertips, breath vast, mouth agape in awe of the eternal skies of possibility. Writing from the body happens prior to the mind of familiar thought, agenda making, patterned conditioning, and control. Writing from the body means bursting forth with a ferocious curiosity, with bright flashes of intuition, keeping time to the songs of blown snow through bent strands of winter wheat. Writing from the body asks you to be edgy and alive, unpredictable, maybe even creatively dangerous. Now is your time to wake up, let go, and get wild against the page!

When we think of our "self," most of us think of our physical appearance—what we see when we look in the mirror and all the baggage we attach to our body. This is the basis of our self-image. But do we see our body as a finite object or as an elaborate process? Do we inhabit our body or does our body inhabit us? Most of us believe the former—our very conception of a self revolves around the physical experience of having and inhabiting a body. After all, our senses are based *in* the body, right? It seems only natural that we conceive of a self through the immediacy of our senses: skin for touch, nose for smell, eyes for sight, mouth and tongue for taste, ears and voice for sound. Our senses create a kind of base reality for us. The totality of our personality, perceptions, knowledge, relationships—ultimately all our conscious experience—seems to emanate from these senses. And even though our entire concept of an individualized self begins in the body as some kind of command center—as our original planet-self *from which* we experience the rest of the universe—what is it that actually makes the body possible?

*

You could write five hundred pages for each of the five senses and you wouldn't make a dent in describing the infinity of sensory experience and display. To become awake means to delve deep into your direct sensory experiences to see them for what they are. Before we go into exploring the ultimate question of the body, let's move more deeply into the experience of our senses in order to move beyond them.

We use our five primary senses every day but mostly in an unconscious and rote kind of way. We don't even think about it. For most of us, sensory impressions directly relate to our preferences and opinions—this is how our senses continue to reinforce our ideas of who we think we are. I like this smell; I don't like that one. I know this taste, touch, smell, whatever; I don't know that one. We are on chronic sensory overload most of the time to the extent that we have literally lost touch with the wonder and brilliance of the immediate world. We are exposed to a constant stream of amazing, bizarre, and wondrous images on the Internet every day. They flit by on our phones, tablets, laptops, desktops, and even on our watches. Screens dominate our public spaces at airports, banks, malls, restaurants, and gas stations, and all of them compete for our attention. We are so busy going from one channel to the next, we don't often stop to revel in much of it with any depth. It doesn't take much of this behavior to numb our senses. They've held experiments in which they've studied young men who watch pornography. After a short period of time, the young men require more imagery to get them aroused. Meanwhile, they experience more difficulty engaging intimately with their partners—that is, generously, open-heartedly, and patiently. And this finding doesn't just apply to pornography. I feel almost physically assaulted trying to sit through almost any kind of big-screen movie previews due to the flashing graphic sensory overload. (I tend to wait outside in the lobby practicing standing meditation until the on-screen explosions and shootings are finished.) Sadly, most of us are dulled and numbed to the beauty and carnality of our immediate surroundings, which makes it difficult to enjoy an authentic connection with the world.

For millions of years, we took in sensory messages at a much slower rate. Waiting in the bush for hours yet sharply alert to the slightest rustle of leaves, thump of feet on earth, breath against sky; our senses were amped for the impending chase. Our lives depended on it. Today, we spend much of our time in front of high-performance screens on which images move faster and appear more real each year. This numbs our overall ability to fully take in, appreciate, and integrate sensory experience. Images move by so quickly and in such great numbers that almost nothing amazes us, but since we're experiencing so much *virtually*, as opposed to *physically*, we rarely integrate these experiences. Hence, they lose their impact and meaning. Over time our sensitivity and sensibility dull, our enchantment and appreciation get worn down. At worst, this results in exhaustion and depression, but most of us regularly get a nagging feeling that something is missing in our lives. And what's missing is authentic connection, deeper emotional engagement, and a more integrated sensory experience.

Sensory experience is primary. It comes before language. The more educated and articulate we become, the more our experience of the senses is augmented by our opinions and beliefs, which are, in turn, shaped by what we expose ourselves to. The language we use is a product of our exposure to certain media. Expose yourself to a manic, high-speed barrage of images and sounds and you are more likely to start to think and believe in certain ways based on that amped-up, surface level of exposure.

I'm not saying that computers, televisions, and smartphones don't have their place. They're wonderful tools in and of themselves, but we need to balance our exposure to them with integrated experiences—I mean experiences in which we slow down, take in sensory impressions, integrate them into our body, and take time to reflect on them for a more complete experience. What happens when we consciously engage in a true practice of observation? When we slow down and make time to experience our senses wide open? Doing so is an act of courage and vulnerability—a softening and opening up to the mysterious complexities of the world. But mostly it's an exciting act of discovery.

As we slow down and open up, we start to realize a whole new depth of experience in the simple act of being. We see and hear things that were there all along, but we simply didn't notice them because we were distracted or spaced out, or numb to their quiet presence. Spiritual teacher Eckhart Tolle teaches a wonderful practice in which he asks participants to pause, sit, and simply *be* with a flower—to simply feel into its presence. Every living being has an essence and emanates an energy field—from the intense presence of great white sharks and grizzlies to the delicate flittering of swallowtail butterflies and wavering wildflowers. Larger beings give off a powerful warning energy, subtler creatures a soft, invitational one. What happens when we tune into the most rarified beings? How about when we connect with the subtler aspects of our innermost selves? Being *with* the quiet nuances of our immediate experience is a practice of reenchantment with the world's miraculousness and beauty—it's a practice of reenchantment with the self.

**TRY THIS**  Tune into each of your senses directly and write from the perspective of that sensory experience—*not* from the person experiencing the sense, but the sense itself, as if it were an animal or a cosmic entity. Write from the inside of the eyes outward, the inner ears outward, the depth beneath the skin outward, the cave of the nose outward, the rippling underbuds of the tongue outward. Write as if you were an ear, an eye, a nose, a tongue, a wrap of skin. Describe your shape and your deepest, most mysterious workings. Speak about how information enters you, how you receive it. Then write how you send this information to the brain and then out into the world.

## SIGHT

As art critic and novelist John Berger writes in *Ways of Seeing*, "Seeing comes before words. The child looks and recognizes before it can speak. But there is also another sense [way in] which seeing comes before words. It is seeing which establishes our place in the surrounding world; we explain that world with words."

By some estimates, at least 80 percent of the information the brain receives comes to us through our eyes. For centuries, the eyes have been called the windows to the soul. They reveal or hide much of who we are. Sometimes waking up is just a matter of seeing things with fresh eyes, as if for the very first time.

I studied photography as an undergrad and graduate student. It took me forever to realize how to slow down and really *see*, which is far more important than operating a camera and developing film. I had strong ideas about what I liked and disliked, what I thought was beautiful and what wasn't, and yet truly seeing certain photographs—the light, framing, and composition—was all about paying attention, becoming more conscious and aware, becoming more *in*sightful in order to become more *out*sightful. All artistic skills and choices are made more profound through the practice of deep seeing. I came to understand that I could also view the world in reflective, dynamic, and symbolic ways. Doing so allowed me to experience layers of perception, emotional complexity, and insight I had never fully contemplated. I began to notice aspects of the landscape and expressions in the faces of people that I had never seen before.

There's a famous picture by French artist and photojournalist Henri Cartier-Bresson of a man leaping from a downed ladder across a puddle on a rain-drenched Parisian street. The gorgeous suspension of time and space in the photo captures something spiritual and transcendent. In the next moment, the man will hit the water and shatter the scene, but when we see him he's at the end of the ladder leaping into the black void of himself. There's an ominous lone figure in the background at the gates of—what? Heaven? Hell? The man, fully committed to the leap, is mirrored by the graphic image of a dancer posted on the far wall. There's also a clock tower in the background, keeping blank time. But all that matters in the photograph is this suspended moment of shadow and light, wonder and sky. It invites us to open up and take it all in; it asks us to slow down and *be* with it.

In this example, I'm referring to a photo, but I could just as easily be talking about a play on stage, a sunset, a bouquet of flowers, words typed out across a page, or your nephew's curious face. What does it mean to truly open yourself to a deeper visual experience of the external? How does doing so affect your intimacy with what's going on *internally*?

## TOUCH

Our entire body is covered with skin—that marvelous organ that allows us to feel millions of sensory impressions a day. Though we don't have time to go into the infinitely complex dynamics of pain sensation and sexuality in regards to touch, I did want to "touch" on a few thoughts around the tactile to inspire you to think about your own experience of touch in new ways. Particularly, let's talk about tactile sensations and how to communicate those to others in writing.

After seventy-nine years in her body, my mother never experienced the extraordinary healing power of a simple massage. She just wasn't a touchy-feely kind of person. Although she became more affectionate later in life, my mother would only hug people she thought were "okay"—that is, sophisticated, intelligent, funny, or rich. And since she was largely absent during my formative years, physical contact was sporadic, random, and subject to my mother's moods. (This was one of the most painful things to write about in my memoir, *Beamish Boy*.) In other words, I didn't have the best modeling about my own sense of touch.

I can't imagine what it must have been like for my mother to live her entire life without the experience of massage, let alone a healing energy-work type of massage. Although it took me years to feel comfortable accepting the type of intimacy that comes from body-work, the experience literally changed my life. The process opened me up energetically, emotionally, and spiritually. To have a complete stranger—one with professional experience, healing intentions, and proper boundaries—rub their hands all over your mostly naked body is an incredible experience that entails trust, openness, and vulnerability, as inevitably sexual and emotional projections, fears, dreams, and complex interpersonal dynamics can arise. To me, this is fascinating, especially when you consider that touch is the most ordinary and natural of human gestures.

Positive touch cultivates connections, deepens social bonds, and expands awareness. Context, intention, and boundaries are everything. We should take care to honor and respect how others choose to relate through touch—everyone has their own sense of what it means to be physically safe and receptive. Some people are huggers—they envelop you in a safe, loving, and strong embrace. Some people would rather keep their distance—they shake your hand or just wave. Some people shake your hand weakly and limply, whereas others grip it with power and conviction. In some cultures, people (even strangers) will kiss one another on the mouth or cheek. Others choose to bow respectfully from several feet away. So, again, context is everything and everyone has their boundaries.

It's been widely documented that children who experience regular loving touch from infancy through their formative years tend to thrive later on. These kids grow up connecting easily to others, remain curious and confident, manage their emotions in a balanced way, concentrate better, and overall feel more safety and peace. On the other hand, it's no surprise that touch-deprivation is associated with loneliness, anxiety, disconnection, fear, withdrawal, and low self-esteem.

Mata Amritanandamayi, popularly known as Amma, is one of the most popular and powerful spiritual teachers living today. She teaches others by hugging them. She says, "My duty is to console those who are suffering," and reminds us that we can express love through compassion, which means viewing the suffering of others as if it were our own. For Amma, such compassion takes the form of physical embrace, and people wait in line for hours just to receive a hug from her. Thousands of people who experience Amma's touch have reported spontaneous healing and immediate feelings of well-being, peace, and love.

What does this all mean for writers? It means that when we open up to tactile sensation, we gain access to a portal of energy and information that allows us to better explore and enrich our creativity. It means that the more we notice, observe, and literally *feel*, the more metaphors and images arise to meet us in heart and mind in the form of words, which can translate our unique experience of intimate contact with the world through our stories, poems, memoirs, and other writing.

## SMELL

Note the difference among the following sentences:

- It smelled terrible!

- It reeked of rotten flesh.

- My scrappy rescue dog, Audrey, munching on a bully stick, fills the room with the scent of wet roadkill.

If I've done my job well, you just got a whiff of foul dog breath and the odor of wet, partially chewed bull penis. Yuck, right? In the third sentence, you get more than a vague description of the smell—you get the beginnings of a scene that entails a personality, a particular tone, and a potential confrontation regarding a horrid smell. Bad smells tend to signal ominous situations, revulsions, and unpleasant memories—all terrific material for novels and memoirs. The lovely smells of flowers, delicate perfumes, and exotic oils and spices trigger other responses. The trick here is to be specific and surprising in order to inspire a visceral response in your readers.

The other day I was walking the aforementioned Audrey on a brutally hot day when I was hit broadside by the smell of rotting flesh. It just hammered me and I was flooded. An arborist had died in this spot a few years prior, and I had just passed the faded wooden cross nailed to a telephone pole that marked the spot. Though I knew the guy had died a couple years prior, I wondered for a second if he was ever taken away. My mind imagined his rotting corpse, partially hidden in the ivy near my feet, so vividly that it felt as if I might trip over his decaying remains. The experience was so potent that I had an immediate sensory reflection on my own death. This is just one example of how smell can set off powerful associations and emotional triggers.

If you've ever walked or bicycled by a dead deer on the side of the road, try to remember that odor right now. Beginning with smell, your imagination can activate multiple senses. For example, remembering the deer, you might also hear vultures nudging their heads sloppily into the soggy carcass. Or the scratch of their claws against the shattered rib cage. Or the deathly slow batting of their wings as they reposition and fan forth the rotten stink as you read these words. If you describe a scene richly enough, what begins as a personal experience transforms into a transpersonal one that has the potential to set off larger contemplations (for example, the temporary nature of your own embodied physical self).

The older my father became, the less acute his sense of smell (and taste, for that matter). Couple that fact with his iron stomach—a wartime hesitancy to "waste not, want not"—and my family rarely got around to cleaning out the fridge. It became a running joke in our household through my high school and college years. Once, a leftover quiche got pushed to the back of the shelf and left there to transform into a sulfurous heap of mold-swaddled egg rot. We ignored it for weeks (months?) until, one day, it finally vanished. My mother quizzed all of us: "What happened to the quiche?"

"Perfectly delicious," my father replied.

> **TRY THIS** Aromatherapy is the use of natural oils found in plants to enhance cognitive, psychological, and physical well-being. It's also an interesting way to engage our sense of smell and write about that experience. Buy an essential oil or choose an aromatic plant from around your house. Inhale the scent and freewrite into whatever comes to mind instantly. Try different smells and note how the scents we prefer inspire different writing than the smells we dislike. Write into the images and associations that arise, and

let the scents take you into hidden memories. List the smells that conjure particularly vivid memories for you. Which inspire more specific details than others? Why might they do so?

## TASTE

"Oh, God above, if heaven has a taste, it must be an egg, with butter and salt, and after the egg is there anything in the world lovelier than fresh warm bread and a mug of sweet golden tea?" That's from Frank McCourt's memoir *Angela's Ashes*. Can't you just taste the egg, warm bread, and golden tea by mere mention? It's making my mouth water just typing it. And here's English novelist Aldous Huxley on the taste of champagne: "Champagne has the taste of an apple peeled with a steel knife." Curious, but surprising and specific. It cuts right to the tongue, so to speak.

I remember the first time I ever tasted a raisin. Not the first time I ever *ate* a raisin, but the first time I ever actually *tasted* one. I was volunteering for the annual summer family retreat at Spirit Rock, when one of the teachers (Jack Kornfield, or perhaps it was Heather Sundberg) led us in a mindful eating exercise. They passed out raisins to everyone in the audience—everyone received one raisin. Then they told us not to do anything with our particular raisin just yet, but simply let it sit in our hands and feel its texture and weight. Finally, after much anticipation, we were allowed to mindfully place the raisin in our mouths. "Don't chew yet!" they warned. "Just let the raisin sit in your mouth, quietly on your tongue." Then they told us to notice everything happening in our mouths as we let the saliva gather and pool, as we rolled the raisin around, as we touched it to the sides, back, and tip of the tongue. Only after all that did they let us bite into the raisin. As we slowly and mindfully chewed it, we allowed the complex release of flavors and noted where we experienced it at different places on our tongues. We noticed the first break of the raisin's skin and how the sharp, plum-sweet flavors transformed over the course of twenty, thirty, fifty chews, until finally experiencing the great mindful cascade of the swallow.

Turns out conscious chewing isn't only spiritually good for you—it's actually good for your digestion, especially when it comes to absorbing nutrients. Conscious eating is a radical act in our "shovel it down" culture, in which we're all too quick to move on to the next taste experience, the next sensation. Conscious eating, mindful chewing, swallowing with presence—all of this, really, is the art of close observation. This means that your experience of eating becomes filled with more detailed depth, more nuanced information that can be translated into the right words to inspire a stomach grumble or saliva spill in your reader who is snuggled up on a random couch halfway around the world.

> **TRY THIS**   Take a raisin and place it in your mouth. Let it sit on your tongue. Be with the experience of the raisin in your mouth. Notice what's there, what's happening. Chew. Chew again, slowly, mindfully. Notice the changes: the flow of saliva, the specific flavors, the different parts of your tongue and how the flavors sit differently upon them. Swallow slowly and mindfully. Notice the aftertaste. Now, grab your notebook and go. Freewrite into your experience of this raisin. How different is it from how you might normally wolf down a raisin, as you would a pill?

## SOUND

This past summer I had the opportunity to hear two amazing bands back to back—Tom Petty with his original band, Mudcrutch, first, and then the Alabama Shakes, both of whom were introduced with opening acts of questionable—what's the right phrase—phonic pleasure? Harmonic commitment? Plain old decent sound?—all in such contrast to the greats. What can one say about Tom Petty? Besides his amazingly brilliant songwriting and arrangements, I was blown away by his humility, grace, and gratitude. His love for the audience was palpable. And if you're not familiar with the Shakes, they're an innovative combination of rhythm and blues, rock, soul, punk, and gospel. And they deliver it all with such joy and spirit that you leave their performance feeling simply ecstatic.

The sounds of a live-music event go far beyond the performance itself. They begin in your head the night before in your quiet anticipation, then pick up during the familiar car-thrum journey to the show, bang around with the street noise as you approach the venue, grow to a buzz and hum of collective audience chatter in anticipation of the main talent, and then culminate in an uncertain roar as the lights go down and the opening band struts on stage. Speaking of which, the opening band for Tom Petty was nothing short of atrocious (bless their creative hearts—no judgment)—but seriously, they were ear-bleedingly bad. I saw people throw their hands over their ears, and I quickly followed suit. Large numbers of us fled to the lobby. The opener for the Shakes wasn't so much overamplified and screechy as monotone and disengaged. Now, how could two of the best acts in show business put up with having terrible bands open for them? Did they not know? Were they trying to accentuate the contrast? Was the price right? Were the openers simply having a bad night? No matter the reason, enduring such sonic discord brought into stark contrast the wild dynamics and variability of sound itself, to say little of our highly nuanced and subjective individual sensibilities that go into such listening.

Are our senses best appreciated in their absence? Perhaps the most direct way to appreciate the depths of sound is to venture into silence. I craved silence after both these concerts and quickly retreated there to assuage the ear ringing. Diminishing input from one of our senses often brings about new insights, a richer experience, and deeper appreciation.

**TRY THIS**   Try these ideas sometime: spend thirty minutes or more in a dark room and pay close attention to what it's like to come back into the light.

There is a remote and wide stretch of beach out at the Point Reyes National Seashore upon which one can roam freely, eyes closed, for great lengths without hitting any other humans or objects, or without veering into the sea. It's a fun exercise to simply walk blind for as long as you can with eyes wide shut, tuning into your other senses for guidance—listening for changes in volume of ocean song, feeling changes of dampness or texture in the sand under foot, or even smelling or tasting the level of salt air on your tongue.

Fast for a day or two and notice how the absence of food heightens the sensitivities of your tongue. I also recommend silent meditation retreats, which highlight subtle vagaries of sound you might not normally hear. If you get quiet enough, you can almost hear the crack and hum of your synapses in action. All your judgments, opinions, and negative self-talk begin to blare much louder than a shitty warm-up band at the Fox Theater. Noting sensations that usually escape our detection allows us to gain distance from our thoughts, which, in turn, gives us the opportunity to form fresh perspectives. A whole new world of sensory information is available to us when we slow down and pay close attention.

Though I'm writing about these sense impressions separately, we don't actually experience the senses in isolation. They work together, blend, overlap, and intertwine. If you want to *see* a rare bird, you have to *listen* to the whole forest. *Tasting* a fine meal requires *smelling* it first. And we don't just *hear* music; we *feel* the bass in our body, and particularly moving melodies can give us goosebumps up and down our arms and legs. In other words, our actual experience is one of synesthesia.

Deeply tuning into the five senses requires practice; it means moving slowly, patiently, and mindfully. Most of us have become increasingly distracted and disconnected from our direct sensory experience. Now is your time to take a break from overstimulation, reengage the natural world, and trust your direct sensory impressions. Your five senses are a gift from the universe—the palette from which your creativity springs forth. All you have to do is redirect your attention and reconvene with the brilliance of your sensory experience, which is, beneath it all, your very nature.

*

We assume that thinking comes from the brain, but the brain is simply a very complex organ that processes trillions of chemical/electrical impulses per second. These complex bits of information come from the far reaches of our body. We often consider the brain and the mind as the same thing, but the mind actually encompasses the whole continuity of thought, experience, emotionality, and physicality. The brain clearly resides in the skull, but where exactly is the mind? Trapped in the mysterious coils of the brain? Woven throughout our entire body? Reverberating farther out into our environment and the physical universe? My answer is all and none of the above. I prefer a broader view that links the mind and heart as one entity of awareness. Together they comprise one space of truth—the home of intuition, insight, wisdom, and love.

We usually think of our body as an individualized object separate from the other bodies out there in a distinctly separate world. Our mainstream reality tells us that I am over here occupying *this* body and you are over there occupying *that* body. After all, the human body seems to possess all the qualities of separateness—that is, being a distinct unit of space and time. But what is a body, really? If I identify *as* a physical body with its constant input of sensations, pains, and pleasures—or even *as* an emotional body with its inevitable emotional swings—then I will necessarily become quite invested in my feelings. In turn, I will create stories about these feelings, which will solidify certain patterns of thought, which will generate deeper beliefs, which will inspire the need to defend these beliefs. That's a simple version of what happens with most of us in daily life.

However, I could just as easily see my sensations and emotions as a *process* happening within, around, or to me. That is, these pulsations of energy and information are not quite the same thing as *me*. Try this one on for size: the *you* that thinks you are *in* the body is not actually in the body; rather, the body is in *you*. What happens when you turn conventional thinking on its head like that? What would change in your experience if you believed that your real *self* is actually consciousness itself, and by consciousness I mean the entire continuity of mind-heart-body-energy that makes up the totality of experience in any given instant? A little abstract, I know, but see if you can think this way for a minute or so: You aren't the small thing trapped in your body you've always believed yourself to be. You're actually everything that's going on—the shining of the sun, the blinking of the stars, the rotation of the planets, the rumbling of thunderstorms, the blossoming of flowers, the sounds of traffic outside your window, the ache in your left foot, the taste of orange rind on your tongue, the sensation of doubt, the pulsation of excitement, the vague darkness of your sleep last night. As twentieth-century Bengali poet Rabindranath Tagore writes in his poem "Stream of Life":

> The same stream of life that runs through my veins night and day
> runs through the world and dances in rhythmic measures.
> It is the same life that shoots in joy through the dust of the earth
> in numberless blades of grass
> and breaks into tumultuous waves of leaves and flowers.

Imagine that the totality—the energy of infinite creation—is the *real* you. Consider the body as just one tiny blip in the midst of this vast sea of the universe. You're not a person (body) experiencing the world but rather the other way around—you are the universe experiencing a body, for a time. It's temporary. Ever notice? The changes, the aging, the deaths of bodies you once knew and loved. What a mystery! What an extraordinary way of reconceiving and reexperiencing the self. So, the next time someone cuts in front of you or steals your spot in a crowded parking lot, ask yourself, who is getting upset? Take a deep breath, feel into the frustration or anger, and watch it dissolve. Instead of becoming overidentified with your thoughts, notice the process—the rise and fall of sensations. The more you practice in this way, the more you can transcend conditioned modes of thinking about yourself, your body, and your creative potential.

This is where writing and meditation come together. As I've mentioned before, writing is one of the most powerful points of focus we have as human beings. Where attention (writing) *goes*, energy *flows*, and results *show* (appear in reality). The key is to be aware of your attention. Where is your mind going? Where is your writing taking you? Be aware of your thoughts, observe the patterns. What are you thinking, what are you believing about this self, this body, in any given moment? How are you reinforcing it or transcending it by your thoughts and beliefs? Writing is an act of creation, and our most primary creation in any given moment involves the self. So, how do you want to write yourself into being?

You might very well ask, "So what?" More to the point, "What am I supposed to do with this? How does thinking of myself as a pattern of energy and information simultaneously happening and exchanging with other patterns of energy and information make me a better writer? And how do I pay my bills with that?" Good questions. Let's start by simply taking it all in, trying it on. I promise that if you genuinely sit with these ideas regularly and repeatedly, if you breathe into this way of seeing and note how (or if) it's true in your own experience, then you will still have to pay your bills. It's just that you'll pay your bills with more ease and grace. You might also notice more patience, more interesting ideas coming to your mind, more insights, and more energy that empower you to write with proficiency and inspiration. And you might start to let go of the fear and tension around any issues that have haunted you your whole life.

We can start by simply becoming more aware of this body. For many of us, doing so can bring up a lot of fear, particularly if we have experienced violence, abuse, or traumatic injury. I recognize the challenge, believe me, but I assure you that it's far from impossible. Your potential for transformation in this lifetime is infinite. Writing is an act of transformation—a courageous act of presence, a gesture of release. And staying present with your sensory experience and bodily sensations is key. Show up for the fear with love and kindness and you'll discover profound change. Sometimes it's too much, and we do need to respect our limitations and pace ourselves over time. I highly recommend working with a professional therapist or energy worker to receive the proper support. It's not easy to express and process stronger emotional and physical sensations. We can start by feeling into our body gently, bringing as much presence and attention as we can in order to let go. By "let go" I mean transcend the limited view of the body, let go of the limiting fear, and release conditioned habits of thought. Ultimately, all we have is this embodied moment, this embodied lifetime, so why not show up as fully as we can? At some point, we'll all have to let go of our body and let it return to the elements from which it came.

*

Speaking of elements, it turns out the human adult body is about 60 percent water. It also happens that the saline and chemical content of a single tear is proportionally the same as a drop of ocean water. Every day we drink in rain, rivers, lakes, and oceans. Water makes it possible for our skin to stretch and flex. It's not metaphoric to say, "I am the ocean." Our bones come from the cooled hearts of volcanoes, as well as the rocks, stones, and soil from our gardens. It's not metaphoric to say, "I am the mountain." We are also beings of light. We need sunlight for healthy skin, bones, and hair. Our eyes and skin take in light, giving rise to heat and the passions of the heart, which have their origins in the core of the sun. In this way, our body is the abode of fire. Every breath is an exchange with the gases of the cosmos. Oxygen and carbon dioxide flow back and forth in conversation with clouds and sky—we are the sky, made of the very air we breathe.

Earth, air, fire, water—the four primary elements of our body and existence itself. Identifying with these entities as our true body gives us a new perspective, a more inclusive understanding of who we really are. We're not a small personality consumed by wants and desires, jolted by fleeting emotional reactions; rather, we're a mysterious elemental process—open and creative, dynamic and evolutionary. What does this all have to do with writing? Everything. Particularly when you write this self into deeper being.

The physical motion of drawing your hand across a page is a primal act of rediscovery. It's a gesture of release and invention, an empowered act of creation. Writing from the body is about reidentifying with your original self; about reaffirming your permeability with the elements. I'm talking about writing into a conversation with the whole cosmos—nothing held back, nothing repressed, nothing denied. Writing from the body is primal and immediate. "First thought, best thought" as the Beat poet Allen Ginsberg advises. Writing as a path to awakening invites you to write from the place beneath familiar thought patterns and rational, conditioned experience. This means writing quick and dirty, dark and scary, fresh and empowering, full of insight and possibility. There's no time for the dusty voices of judgment and critique, no room for teacherly correctives. I'll say it again: it's time to be edgy and alive. The moment has come to be creatively unpredictable. Time to wake up and write into your unique elemental bodily wildness, to discover the wisdom of wildness within!

What happens when you think of yourself and your writing as white bird wings waving against stormy blue-gray clouds, elk hoofprints trailing through the snow, a set of mountain lion tracks set in soft mud, bare oak branches scripting forth a winter sky, the chatty ripple patterns whipped up on the surface of a once calm lake, or the high horsehair clouds being drawn by mountain peaks? Your body is the earth's body, the sky's body—one body, one writing. It's how you stroll down a beach, your footprint pattern left behind against a fleeting page of earth. Your writing is the landscape writing itself through you. It's the deer writing, the branches writing; water, light, and windripple writing through that field of possibility that is you.

### → *Standing Meditation Exercise*

Here's an excellent way to reconnect to your body.

Keeping a pen and notebook nearby, stand up and let your hands rest easily by your sides. Close your eyes gently and keep your feet flat on the floor. Take a single deep breath and exhale slowly. Then take two more deep, slow breaths. Keep your eyes closed and really feel your body breathing. Notice the rhythm and depth of your breath.

Let your shoulders relax. Breathe into any areas of tension in your body. Bring your feet together so that your ankles touch softly. Breathe in and out. Now try to bring yourself to an absolute still point, but keep your attention on the breath. After a few moments, you might notice a gentle swaying and your body's natural inclination to correct. Let your body move slightly as if it were a tree, but remain rooted in the nourishing earth. Above, you converse with the wind and breathe into the sky; below, you stand firmly while pulling up minerals and water.

Breathe deeply, keep your eyes closed, and adjust your feet until they are about the width of your shoulders apart. Now bring your attention to your feet. Feel them rooted in the ground. Visualize the bones of your feet. Start with the smallest bones in your toes and imagine them connecting to your larger foot bones. Then visualize those attaching to your ankle bones and see how ankles join tibias and fibulas, and how those meet your knees. Visualize your kneecaps and joints, see how the femurs rise into your hips, your hips into your spine, and see how the vertebrae climb up your spine in a natural curve like flowers. And now notice how your spine branches out into the rib cage and visualize those bones curving around and coming together at the sternum, branching off at your clavicles to the joints at your shoulders. See how the bones of your arms connect at your elbows and reach down to your wrists. Visualize the nimble bones of your hands, all the way to the tips of your fingers. Now come back up to your wrists, now up the arms to your elbows, now back to your shoulders, and see the scapula. Now see how your spine rises and connects at the skull. Visualize your skull, your eye sockets, your jaw bone and teeth.

Now imagine that you can step away. Pan out to see your whole skeleton, the scaffolding of the self, the framework that keeps you upright and sturdy. Look at the whole array of the magical bones of your body. Take a deep breath and exhale. Your bones are the minerals from the mountains, the rocks and stones, the soil from your garden. These bones are the very earth you stand upon. Take another deep breath.

Breathe now into the liquid self that lives between your bones and throughout the rest of your body. This requisite fluid—blood, mucus, sweat, neurotransmitters, tears—is the ocean. It's the same as the creeks, rivers, lakes, and rain. Breathe all this in.

Now bring your attention to the center of your chest to your heart. Feel the power and heat there. Appreciate how warmth permeates your body. The fire of your love and determination is the fire of the sun. Sunlight ignites your energy and creativity. Take another deep breath in, then exhale.

Now notice your breath. Visualize the oxygen and carbon dioxide in constant exchange. Your breath reaches into the atmosphere, pulling in the clouds. You inhale, bringing the sky within you. Exhale. You are the vastness that surrounds you. Now breathe deeply again.

These are the elements of your primal, original being: earth, air, fire, and water. You are composed of cosmic collisions—you are the origins of the stars. Breathe for a couple of minutes into that expanded sense of self. Now open your eyes slowly and sit down.

Pick up your notebook and pen. Let's go straight into writing.

———◆———

### Writing Exercise: The Elemental Self

Let's freewrite into our elemental selves. Choose one of the four elements and write from the perspective of that element. Take it on as an identity. Don't think too much about it. Feel into your body and let the words come from within, from your elemental self. Time yourself for ten minutes.

If you get stuck, use the following questions to guide you. Try to be as specific as you can.

- What color are you?

- What do you look like?

- Where do you dwell?

- What emotions do you experience as this element?

- How do you move about?

- How do you like to express yourself?

- What is it like to see through the eyes of fire (or dance as a molecule of air, etc.)?

You can also jump-start your writing by filling in the blanks of the following sentences:

The *earth* within me is made up of (choose a particular dynamic material) _____ that (strong verb) _____.

(Example: The earth within me is made up of crystal flowers that radiate scarlet facets of mood and mind . . .)

The *fire* within me (strong "personified" verb) _____ and reminds me to _____.

The (color) _____ *air* (active verb) _____ within me like (simile) _____.

The (body of *water*) _____ (strong verb) _____ through my _____ as if _____.

—➤◆◆—

# 11

# November
## {Reflection}

*Editing and the Art of Revision*

I t's November now. Time to turn further inward and metabolize our newly empowered and emboldened sense of self. Time to reflect and re-vision. I'll start us off with a story about reflecting on life and re-visioning our default emotional reactions and responses, and I hope the application to writing is evident.

My friend Margaret is a beautiful, athletic force of nature. She rides her bike constantly, and not just to commute. Margaret rides because she prefers bikes to cars; she rides to save money and to assuage the effects of global warming; she rides for health and well-being; she rides because it makes her happy. In other words, she rides for love.

A couple of years ago Margaret rode her bike to South America. She originally described the idea quite casually, in the same way I might announce a trip to the store to fetch a carton of milk. And Margaret wasn't merely riding to the top of South America, to Colombia; Margaret journeyed seven thousand miles from San Francisco to the very southern tip of South America, to Tierra del Fuego.

Five years ago, during a rare journey on foot through India and Nepal, Margaret finally arrived in Kathmandu to prepare for a trek in the Himalayas. She had been saving up for months for the trip. Her husband, Cody, met her in Nepal to "fatten her up," since Margaret had lost so much weight in her travels through India. At the time,

Cody lived in Abu Dhabi, where he would return after Margaret left on her trek. Before she left for the Himalayas, she wanted to book a flight to Abu Dhabi to reunite with Cody for a while.

According to Margaret, part of managing money in the developing world requires traveling light. Margaret only needed about $200 worth of small bills and coins in rupees to pay for lodging and food for the next month of trekking. When she booked her flight at a travel agency in Kathmandu, a teenage street kid who had been awkwardly hovering about, offering to interpret, told Margaret that he'd be happy to get her ticket for her that afternoon. However, Margaret would need to pay the full price for her flight now. Understandably, Margaret was suspicious. They negotiated tensely, until she agreed to pay half now and the rest when she picked up her flight ticket later that day. They had a deal!

That afternoon a nagging sickness returned (she had been ill off and on for weeks) and hit Margaret hard—she couldn't even leave the hotel room. So she asked Cody to walk to the travel agency, pay for the rest of her ticket, and find a way to break down $200 in large bills that the ATM had issued her. This latter task would probably be an undertaking—Kathmandu is typically full of tourists trying to make change. Regardless, after a few delirious hours Cody came back to the hotel room with the flight document in hand. Margaret was surprised and delighted. However, when she asked if Cody was able to change the $200 for smaller bills, he offhandedly mentioned that he had entrusted that task to the same friendly teenage boy who helped Margaret earlier that day.

She fell silent in disbelief. For months, Margaret had hidden her money tightly against her body as she traveled through India. She had reacted with reasonable suspicion to anyone who approached her, especially anyone who offered to make a "deal" with her. Margaret is tall, blond, and white—in other words, she stood out in India. Wherever she went, people begged her for money, pulling on her clothes and bags. She tried to hand out food and small change on occasion, but she wore all her essential documents and most of her money tight to her skin. And now Cody, her trusted husband, had given the $200 bookmarked for her thirty-day Himalayan trek to some poor street kid in Kathmandu.

She screamed at him. "My money is gone!" she yelled. "How could you be so naive?"

Meekly, Cody replied, "He's a good kid. He'll do what he promised. I believe in him."

Margaret continued to scream at Cody until her screaming turned to sobbing. She'd been dreaming of this trip for years and now it was gone. She buried her face into her pillow and cried for the rest of the day.

A few hours later, Cody made his way to the travel agency. He met the street kid at the appointed time. And then he returned with a bag of change not one rupee short of Margaret's $200.

To say the least, Margaret was glad to be proven wrong. She was also deeply humbled. Truth be told, Margaret really had liked the kid, but she wasn't a fool. Two hundred dollars would go a long way in Kathmandu for someone accustomed to living off a dollar or two for days or weeks. She just didn't think the kid could resist the temptation.

There's more to the story, of course. Sohan (the kid) and Margaret have kept in touch on Facebook. He's grown into a fine young man. He told her of his dreams to leave his hometown and see the larger world someday.

But then the earthquake hit. It destroyed Sohan's home. He and his family struggled to find food, water, and basic shelter. They were considered lucky, as the earthquake had killed over eight thousand people in Nepal alone. Entire villages were flattened. The quake rendered hundreds of thousands of people homeless.

Through Facebook, Margaret found and donated to a GoFundMe account set up to help Nepali survivors. And then, somehow, Margaret contacted Jay, a neighbor here in California who happened to be traveling in Kathmandu, and asked him to check in on Sohan. Jay found him, and then without knowing anything about their story of the money exchange, he donated $200 to Sohan's family. Sohan broke into tears, overwhelmed with gratitude.

I love this story for a lot of reasons. It reminds me of the deep connection we can have to people tens of thousands of miles away, despite our differences in economic means, cultural traditions, and values. When they suffer, we suffer. But I also love this story because it reminds me how we can so easily get stuck in a mind-set of lack and limitation. Because we don't see the bounty and possibility before us, our tendency is to engage others with suspicion and distrust, particularly if they are "other." Of course, sometimes it's good to be suspicious and a little on guard, but we overdo it. We need to open a little more to the inherent good in people.

At every moment we have the ability to review—to re-vision—any given situation and our reactions to it with a larger sense of possibility. Sometimes it takes a friend, partner, or complete stranger to knock us out of distrust and suspicion. And we often need that extra bit of help to *edit* our default emotional responses.

> **TRY THIS** Can you think of a time when you freaked out with an immediate reactive emotional response based on patterning and judgment, fear or doubt, and then thought, "Hey, wait a minute—is this the whole story? Is this even true?" Identify one of these moments and write into it, re-visioning the instant when you realized something larger, a greater truth and different possibility. What was your response in retrospect? Can you rewrite that now to set you up for a different future reality?

Let's cut to the chase. When it comes to editing our prejudices and emotions or editing our writing, the process isn't easy. In fact, editing can be humbling, grueling, mind-numbing, repetitive, redundant, and rigorous work. And yet editing is the heart and soul of writing; editing in all its guises is a transformative act of surprise, discovery, and insight. To quote Elizabeth Gilbert from *Big Magic*, "Art is a crushing chore and a wonderful privilege." What happens when we allow both things to be true, in art *and* life simultaneously?

The protagonist of my recent novel, *Brooklyn, Wyoming*, is hiding out in western Wyoming, living in a school bus under an assumed name. He's been on the run for fifty years and is currently drinking himself to death in an unsuccessful effort to erase his troubled past.

He's an amateur songwriter. One night he starts obsessing over some Neil Young lyrics and gets inspired to write. He writes and writes, until he eventually runs out of paper, so he starts writing on his kitchen table, on the curtains, on the walls, and on the windows:

> I got sucked into writing on all the surfaces in the bus, and then it became a project. I had a bunch of paint left over from the refurbishing, and permanent markers that wrote on any surface. It soon became an obsession . . . at a certain point, I knew I wouldn't stop until I could no longer see out the windows, until there was no surface left unworded . . . at the right time of day, word-shadows would coat me as sunlight streamed through the windows; they would rub off on me as I wiped my hands on an embroidered towel. If I picked up a pot holder, the words would bake into my hands as I cooked. I wrote on or had all the mugs and glasses printed so that words and their meanings splashed into me when I drank, like the voices from a river. Maybe I thought my brief flourish of what the textbooks I think call "hypergraphia," might alleviate the hurt, mollify the demons of loneliness and regret, somehow cover my tracks. Maybe it was a way for me to rewrite the past, do a little editing, as it were. God knows I needed editing.

If all writing is rewriting, then maybe all living is reliving. And hopefully that means progressive bursts of growth arise with every challenging experience we navigate, successfully or otherwise. An Eastern sage once said that *we are our thoughts*. Thoughts become words, which express themselves as actions in our lives. In this way, we are language itself, played out in physical form. Editing our writing, editing our life—it's all one story.

What is editing, really? If we take the term literally, *revision* means to revisit our senses—to resee, resmell, rehear, retaste, and refeel into our direct experience with more depth and insight. In re-visioning, we bring a fresh awareness to every open moment of the page *and* to every open moment of our life. That's how we improve and evolve.

Every time we sit down to meditate, we open up space to shed our conditioning, even if by an unnoticeable amount. Every time we watch our breath and extend kindness to ourselves, we allow in more brilliance, more compassion. Practice helps us enter a space of vulnerability, and this illuminates our heart and soul a little bit more. We can use this light to better see our current or past creations in order to experience them from new angles, with new insight, and perhaps with a little less resistance. With writing, this might take the form of dropping a word, sentence, paragraph, or chapter. It might look like adding a word, sentence, paragraph, or chapter. It might mean throwing similes across the page like a fistful of stars into the night sky. We might create an entirely new character based on the dream we had last night. Such is the magic of being a more open and creative soul—it's a constant process of discovery and adventure. From moment to moment, we never know what we might learn. And the more curious and permeable we become, the more the knowledge and wisdom of the universe comes streaming into our body, heart, and mind.

The key word is *process*. In the previous chapter we looked at how our body and the self we associate with that body only exists in process. Well, the sooner we can wrap our mind around writing as a *process*—that is, an adventurous journey—instead of a *product*, the sooner we can get into the work of writing as an act of discovery. We can let go of perfectionism and surrender to the journey of instructive failures that transform into flowers of success as we step forward into process. Doing so, we connect with all that we have to share with the world, instead of getting stuck in the rut of self-doubt and judgment. Editing is about reviewing every written word and considering another way of writing it out. When I begin writing, I work with general and abstract ideas, just to get words on the page. However, editing requires keener attention, personalized specificity, new information, and brighter ideas that, hopefully, offer a spark of lasting wisdom.

*All writing is rewriting* makes the process sound arduous, but there's genuine magic in watching words travel from general abstraction to specificity. We shape and sculpt our writing over time and watch in awe as our unique voice shines through with nuance and insight. The art of revision begins with humility. It means surrendering to the fact that we don't know it all, especially right out of the gate. Thinking that we do know it all or believing that our first thoughts and first drafts are "good enough" can be disastrous—it's lazy thinking. Have you ever heard the adage "Good enough seldom is"? We can always improve our writing.

I once attended a poetry reading in San Francisco in which the great poet and art critic Bill Berkson got up to read a piece of his that had been published in *Postmodern American Poetry: A Norton Anthology*. Instead of reading the poem as it was published in the anthology, Bill pulled out a recently edited copy from his pocket and read that version. I was stunned. I mean, hadn't the official poem already been published? And not just in any anthology, but in the hallowed *Norton Anthology*. I had always assumed once a poem was published in a journal (and especially an anthology), the editors and tastemakers had cast their spell—you were now accepted into the kingdom; the work was done.

I submitted a lot of poems for publication, and I sent a large number of them out impatiently, possibly even prematurely. Even so, some of those were accepted by journals for publication. (Literary journals are often forums for new work by writers as a step in the process toward future publication in anthologies or books, with the acknowledgment that their work will eventually be edited and evolve.) Since I hadn't given some of the poems their due on my end, I still had nagging, unresolved feelings about them. Following Bill's example, when I finally went back and edited those poems, I felt better about them *and* myself as a writer. Doing so changed how I saw writing as a whole—that is, I began to view writing as a process and journey rather than a product and destination. Of course, not everything requires editing. It's also true that sometimes your first thought is your best thought. You occasionally get lucky, and a spontaneous freewrite turns out to be a stroke of uneditable genius. In my experience, this happens quite rarely—at least for me. It's also true that some work will stay just as it is. Exhausted by your tinkering, the words settle into a certain level of satisfaction and completion. Others passages nag and moan like bored children, continually asking to be petted and complimented. You can tweak these for all of eternity, but they'll never quite settle.

Thank god for the magic and mystery of intuition, and for the magic and mystery of professional editors who give us insight and perspective. Sometimes, especially during the early stages of our writing, we don't necessarily know what's good or bad for us. Are we being too hard on ourselves? Not hard enough? What's the best way to make any given paragraph shine? That's when it's time to let an outside perspective in.

Remember, however, that editing is an active process on your end. Keep reading and rereading your work. Then read it out loud to yourself, your dog, and anyone who will listen. Then have a trusted reader take a look and give you constructive feedback. At a certain point along the journey, you have to trust your intuition—things click into place and the writing just *feels* right. My process includes multiple rounds of edits until the writing is about as good as I can get it. Only then do I share it with my official readers (at least three) before I send the work to my agent and editor at the publishing house. If you don't have an agent or editor, you can hire a professional, but make sure they have the credentials you're looking for. If you want to place your work with one of the major publishers, hire a freelance editor who has a track record of working on books published with those companies. Ask for references and try the editor out with a small piece of writing before committing to a major project such as an entire manuscript.

\*

The writing and editing process takes discipline. *All writing is rewriting* is the definition of discipline. How does one *get* discipline? I once believed that discipline was one of those things you were born with, or maybe you got it from someplace such as military school. I grew up in a lefty, pacifist household with a dictatorial German nanny. The only discipline my parents expressed involved cocktails and dinnertime; Miss Hedy's version of discipline was rigid, unkind, and oppressive. You can imagine the confusion and subsequent rebellion. Needless to say, I have bad associations with discipline—I grew up rejecting it and thinking of it as some type of genetic trait that I lacked. Even so, my career and spiritual path require discipline, so I have developed an appreciation for regimen, pattern, and self-control. It's all a question of balance and degree.

For the longest time I dreamed of becoming a writer, but I didn't have the self-worth to believe that my ideas mattered, so I didn't get off my ass and take any action. Here's another equation for you:

*Low Self-Esteem + No Discipline = No Writing*

Gradually I noticed that the people who make things happen in the world—people who change the world for the better, people who actually make their dreams come true—have discipline. I began to understand that it's not so much that they *have* discipline, but rather that they *create* it. But how? I was puzzled about this for years until I realized that these people create discipline from within. Within? Within *what*? I didn't even know there was a *within* until I started meditating. I was so conditioned to look for answers on the outside that it never occurred to me that all knowledge, insight, love, possibility, and (hello!) discipline comes from within. I eventually learned that discipline has nothing to do with comfort, ease, and preference—that is, what I'd most like to do in the moment. Discipline has nothing to do with fulfilling sudden pleasures or satisfying cravings for sex, food, love, attention, or buying bright shiny things off the Internet.

Discipline has everything to do with service—to self, to others, to community and society, to higher purpose and divine inspiration. Our level of happiness depends on how much we give to others and how much kindness we express. Happiness also comes from a personal sense of completion and competence. When we follow through with a project and complete it, we feel a sense of usefulness and pride. I'm not knocking pleasure. Pleasure certainly has its place. The problem, however, is that pleasure is so damn fleeting, and we can chase it into the dark of confusion. I invite you to see how this is true in your own experience. Personally, I get so much more lasting happiness from bringing my loved one a latte in bed or volunteering at a food bank than I do bailing on a writing session to watch *Portlandia*.

Having discipline simply means that we practice facing our urges and resistances directly. Discipline takes serious awareness and patience. It's a combination of *intention* and *attention*. First, we feel the sincere desire (intention) to write that article, story, book, play, poem, or novel; then we focus (attention) on meeting that desire—moment by moment, day by day. Discipline requires repetition, reminding, and reacting to lesser influences in a way that fosters our greater good. There's no force outside of you that can give you discipline. Sure, you can be inspired and motivated by others through reading, listening, and watching, but their passing influence will not sustain you over time, especially when you encounter your demons of resistance.

In other words, you must actively cultivate the practice of discipline mentally, physically, and—most importantly—spiritually. When resistance rears its familiar head, you redirect its energy over and over again. You divert it mentally with supportive thoughts and affirmations. You rechannel it physically by stepping away from the fridge, going for a hike, stretching, and moving. You redirect it spiritually by taking time to calm your mind, drop everything, and breathe. I recommend meditating in silence every day. It also helps to go for a mindful walk and reset your intention to shut up and write (or edit) not later but right *now*.

## Meditation on Editing

Center yourself in your breathing body, knowing in this moment there is nothing to do, no knowledge to gather or remember, no proper way to breathe, nothing to get right or control. You are simply sitting and noticing the experience of your breathing body, letting all tension and expectations go. There is nothing to figure out or fix—you are here to allow everything to be just as it is. As you breathe, allow your mind to rest in an open state. Let thoughts be thoughts, sensations be sensations. Just rest here, breathing through all that arises in heart and mind with full awareness, allowing yourself to be bathed in silence and attuned to the reality of the present moment, breath by breath. Enter into the silence of yourself and reflect on your current momentary state of being.

After a few minutes you might notice yourself getting distracted by thoughts and ideas, feelings and plans. As you notice this in yourself or at the sound of my voice (on the audio), take a moment to return to your breathing body. After twenty to forty minutes of silence and at the sound of the bell, check back in on another moment of reflection, noting how you are now. What is your current state of being in open reflection? Be aware of the changes without assigning judgment, positive or negative. Notice this new state and anything new that arises as a bodily experience. Let these sensations bring you further into the present. Creation is happening right now. In the present. Feel into your body as it is born anew in every moment through breath, sound, and energy.

---

→ *Editing Writing Exercise*

1. Using the prompt "That first summer I ever _____," freewrite by hand for fifteen minutes. Don't think too much about it—just set the clock, fill in the blank, and go. If you are still flowing when the timer goes off, feel free to keep writing until the energy subsides.

2. Now go back and read through what you just wrote. Highlight, underline, or put an asterisk next to at least three lines, phrases, or words that feel bright, interesting, or surprising to you.

3. Next, rewrite the entire piece by hand. Even if you typically freewrite on a keyboard, print out what you've written and use pen and paper. If you're hesitant or resistant to do this, consider this exercise an opportunity to experiment. Add at

least three sensory details that describe the features of a person, object, or aspect of a specific place. Include color, shape, smell, tactile experience, sound, and even taste. If adding three sensory details comes easy for you, include three more and become even more specific.

4. Add at least two metaphors or similes. (See chapter 4.)

5. Personify some inanimate object or emotion in your piece. (See chapter 4.)

6. Replace three verbs with vibrant, buzzing action words. Exaggerate and be hyperbolic! Don't worry if it doesn't fit the overall tone of your piece—this is practice.

7. Rewrite this piece a third time. As you do so, delete (cross out or erase) any dead, boring, or useless sentences or phrases that don't add surprise or energy. Also remove anything that is redundant or doesn't fit the main intent of the piece.

8. Now type it up. In this round, clean up your punctuation and spelling. Look for places to add more detail, link sentences, remove flat lines, and fill out scenes and characters with specificity.

9. Read the original version. Then read the version you just typed out. Notice the differences—the evolution, the transformation.

10. Celebrate! You've just activated your creative genius in practice, process, and proficiency!

# Winter

# 12

# December

## {Sanctuary}

*Writing, Living, Dying, and Becoming . . . Full Circle*

We have come full circle, arriving at the sanctuary of the self. Brimming with insight, knowledge, and wisdom, we glow bright with truth. We have journeyed back to the inner sanctum—our inner sacred space, our sacred refuge, our space of surrender, of grace and becoming. Taking all we've learned this entire "year" through reading, writing, and being—all we've conjured, gathered, contemplated, doubted, dreamed, and discovered—it's time to give back and let go once again, breath by breath, moment by moment. December is our time to descend back down into the depth and dark nurturance of the unknown. This is our time to die to the old in order to birth forth the new. We are beings of return, rediscovery, and rebirth through the profound transformation of death.

Who were you prior to your birth? Who were you prior to name, shape, personality, and character? Who are you, really, but a field of possibility, an open network of potentiality, an expansive conduit of energy, information, and love?

*

My father was born in 1914 at the beginning of World War I. He was nine years old when my grandfather took him to his first college football game in upstate Connecticut. They traveled by train. At some point in the journey, father and son stepped outside on the small platform together to enjoy some fresh autumn air. They were holding hands when the train made a sudden jerk at a bend. My grandfather lost his balance. His hand yanked from my father's to catch himself, and he fell over the railing to his death in the flickering tracks below.

My father was a conscientious objector during World War II. They sent him to build roads in the Appalachian Mountains, made him work as a ship hand transporting horses back and forth from Italy, and subjected him to germ warfare medical experiments at a lab in Tennessee. Although my father was too old to serve in Korea and Vietnam, he protested both wars. His second wife hung herself from the heating pipes of their apartment in Greenwich Village when she was still in her twenties. My half brother David, still in his twenties at the time, found her. David disappeared into the remote badlands of Wyoming for twenty years in the late seventies and gradually drank himself to death. I was in high school then. I don't remember a funeral. Dad remarried three more times before meeting my mother in 1960. They were married for almost forty years. Dad went to architecture school, practiced off and on for twenty years without ever securing a major project. He did, however, redesign the extraordinary house of his dreams, the one that I grew up in, the one he lost in the economic crash of the late 1970s. During all of this, my father also cared for his schizophrenic sister until her death. And however remote and emotionally disconnected he was (one can certainly understand why), he managed to raise my two sisters and me through endless challenges we posed muddling through our dramatic reactions to a chaotic and violent household. Throughout it all, my father pressed on.

Who was this man who endured such grief and tragedy? Who are any of us, really, with all the slings and arrows that pierce an ordinary life? Where's the sanctuary in it all?

My father died three weeks after 9/11, on the day the United States invaded Afghanistan. No one has ever heard of him. You won't find him on Google, he made no major contributions per se (beyond his quiet donations to civil liberties and antiwar causes), but he lived rather dramatically and endured. There are only four people alive who ever think of him—his first son, Richard, my two sisters, and me. Otherwise, it's as if he never existed. My father was arguably the most important person in my life, but he was also the most fleeting and unknown. He was in his midfifties when I was born and had already lived several lives. I was his last child. He was tired, exasperated, and altered by personal tragedies and social discord (Vietnam, the assassinations of Martin Luther King Jr. and Robert Kennedy, etc.). By the time I was born, my father was already too broken to fully engage his children, but he did persevere. I owe my life to him (and my mother, of course).

Around the time of my father's death, I kept a poetry journal that I eventually compiled into a tiny book of fragmented poem-sections called *Time Pieces*. One reads:

> 45 geese on the lawn
> 116 on the river
> 1 child running
> chases the lawn
> clean

Visiting him in the hospital, I wrote about the fleeting memories of childhood, about a single great blue heron on the Hudson River, about Dad's white beard pressed flat like bleached, wind-beaten winter grasses by the translucent green oxygen mask. I wrote about his lungs rattling like a crippled cricket, about the tinted hospital windows, about the setting sun crinkling up the surface of the river—about the river (of life itself) withering away within my father. He died four days after my birthday. It was a gorgeous autumn day. When I returned to California, my best friend, Todd, composed a beautiful song from the poem. Todd sang the song to me and I felt as if I might just dissolve into nothingness from the grief and beauty of it all. It wasn't my words as much as Todd's voice, guitar arrangement, and the pure kindness that went into his honoring a man he had never even met.

What do we do with death? Of the infinitely empty answers to that question, here's what I have come to believe: We surrender into the unknown. We appreciate the complex majesty of our life and the mysterious lives around us, of the ones we love. We lie softly on the sacred earth and breathe deep of its mysterious insistence on death, destruction, rebirth, and beauty. We make art. We go within to feel the fathomless lands of the self, loving fully and with open abandon.

*

Entering the sanctuary of death is mostly about acceptance. It's about entering into a different relationship with the truth of being—temporary in this body, in this time, yet eternal in spirit. Our relative time is limited. We never know how much we have. All we really "have" is this moment, and yet every moment carries within it the taste of eternity, just as every drop of the sea contains the entire ocean. And so we are called to awaken to this moment's miraculous gifts and challenges.

Writing into loss, grief, and death can be life enhancing. We might think it will be morbid and depressing, but writing into the dark unknown can surprisingly spit you back out into the light. Since I began writing prose, I have not stopped writing about my dead parents. And I can't describe how much this process has helped me grow in terms of appreciation, understanding, insight, and love.

Did you ever see the movie *Touching the Void*? Two best friends are climbing in the Peruvian Andes when one of them falls. Fortunately, the rope holds and prevents him from plunging a thousand feet down to certain death. Unfortunately, he is dangling over a cliff with no way to reconnect to his partner above. It's getting colder and darker, and options melt away like so much sun-touched snow. The friend on top eventually realizes that to save either of them, which means himself, he will need to cut his friend loose. He can't save his friend; all he can do is save himself. After much anguish, he finally wills himself to cut his friend free and leave him to die. His friend plummets downward. Surprisingly, he doesn't die on impact, but slides into a crevasse. He survives the fall with a broken leg but is fifty feet down with icy walls on either side and no possibility of climbing his way out. And yet he stares longingly up at the light trying to figure a way up and out. With no remaining options, he counterintuitively heads down into the dark, deeper into the crevasse, hoping for a way out. Every movement sends pain shooting through his wrecked leg. Still, he crawls on blindly. He can barely drag himself any farther when he rounds a corner in the ice and sees a faint light. He pulls his body to the light, inch by painful inch, until a gap in the glacier appears. He crawls out of the gap in disbelief. He somehow drags himself a couple miles back to the base camp, where he finds his friend, crying in his soup and convinced he's looking at a ghost.

Writing is like that sometimes. Living, too. We must cut the metaphoric rope, free-fall to our death, and crawl our way out by going farther down into the black unknown. Although it's contrary to our inclinations and common sense, *down* is where we find the opening. When things sometimes feel bleak and hopeless, that's where we find the light.

> **TRY THIS** Write the words *death* and *sanctuary* at the top of your notebook. What does *sanctuary* mean to you? What is its relationship to the word *death*? Why is the word *eat* embedded within the word *death*? What happens when we bite into the tough unknowing bones of death? Do we then at least get a chance to taste the marrow of the light? Freewrite for fifteen minutes into your experience of these two words. Don't think, just write.

I'm about to ask you to go into the dark with a little more depth. The concluding writing exercise might be the most challenging one yet, so I want to share a related personal story before I go.

Remember the psychedelic therapy group I mentioned in chapter 1? One of the core activities I participated in were weekend workshops (usually group trip-fests) in remote locations with a little "processing" tossed in. One of these workshops, centered on *the dark side*, was held (for once without "medicines," a.k.a. drugs), appropriately enough, near the summit of Mount Diablo in Northern California. There were about twenty of us, all men, circled around a fire late one night. Our leader, my therapist (yes, he had a PhD in psychotherapy, with an emphasis on the *psycho*), was dressed all in black and wearing a hood. Next to him stood a couple of henchmen, with arms crossed, whom none of us had ever seen before. Every one of us was spooked to the gills. Our leader began by having us write down on tiny pieces of colored paper the most important aspects of our lives—people we love the most, our favorite childhood pets, places that shaped us emotionally, our dreams about the future—anything we cherished whatsoever. He then made us crumple up those pieces of paper and toss them into the fire.

The ritual hit me hard. I trembled with emotion as I watched those written representations of everything I held dear burn up in the fire. My therapist must have noticed my reaction because, after a long, uncomfortable silence, he pointed across the circle at me, arm thrust out like a bayonet, and shouted, "You! Any last words?" I froze with terror. After a tense pause, he waved to his henchmen. "Take him!" he yelled.

His goons grabbed me, threw a hood over my head, tossed me into a burlap sack, dragged me into the forest, and tied me to a tree. I have never been so terrified in my life. I begged them to let me go. Weeping, I hoped that it was all a joke, a prank of some sort, and they would be back for me soon. But as the minutes ticked by, I began to panic. I could hear coyotes howling, owls shrieking, and wild boar snorting somewhere out there in the dark. The terror was unbearable. I watched my whole life flash in front of me as if it were a jittery filmstrip of memory. Through my tears, I said goodbye to everyone I loved.

Time ticked by painfully slow. I went back and forth between anticipating my release and anticipating my impending death. At some point I felt into my breathing, a couple heartbeats, and soon realized I was still very much alive. The more I turned inward, the more gratitude proliferated within me for simply being alive. Up to that point in my life, I had never experienced such aliveness—such vitality and presence. And in that moment I made a vow: *If I ever get untied from this tree I will devote myself wholeheartedly to creativity, to loving, and to serving others.* Also, I promised myself, I would quit this psycho group!

And I did. At the time I was still at the Art Institute, flailing about with photography, when I was invited (by my art history professor and late great poet Bill Berkson) to the poetry reading that changed my life. It was a reading to celebrate the release of *Postmodern American Poetry:*

*A Norton Anthology* edited by Paul Hoover. That night I heard a line of poetry that literally changed my life:

> The poet builds a castle on the moon
> Made of dead skin and glass.

That's from Jack Spicer's "Imaginary Elegies," and when I heard Paul Hoover read that line I felt something click in my heart. That wondrous image peeled me wide open. For the past two years, I had been struggling through graduate school, lost and unmotivated, and I knew in that moment I was supposed to be doing something other than photography—I was meant to do something with *words*. I, too, would build my "castle on the moon" made of wild metaphors, of enigmatic and passionate words. I wasn't sure what Spicer's words meant, but I wanted to be part of that imaginative continuum of writing. At the same time, I somehow intuitively knew that this was my key to living as a more conscious, compassionate human being. Something had truly shifted during my terrifying ordeal. Crazy as it was, it had worked. I was now reborn into the light of creativity and possibility.

\*

How can we contact a primal state of being that lies beneath all our conditioning and projections? How can we access our deathless place of creativity and possibility? Can we die to the old stories in our life (as well as the patterned legacy of our parents' and ancestors' lives), to the ones that no longer serve us, and wake up to a new potentiality that is available to us through the journey of mindfulness and writing?

Yes, we can! Yes, *you* can! May this book be your support, your inspiration, your guide. This is your chance to write forth a new script for your life, to write forth the truth of who you really are—through that short story, journal, novel, memoir, play, movie script, or book of poems that you have always wanted to write. From this moment forward, may your writing practice be your sanctuary. May it truly enrich the full depth and experience of your life. Remember, you are not your story—you are an open poetic field of possibility, a creative genius, a brilliant writer. The invitation is to wake up and write, and now is your time!

→ *A Meditation on Death*

Settle yourself into your immediate experience and presence of the breathing body by following the instructions in the first chapter's introductory meditation. Take a few breaths inward, release any obvious tension, and then settle into the natural rhythm of your breathing.

Breathe into your experience of the word *death*. What's it like to simply read or hear that word? What gets stirred up in your mind? Allow whatever is there to be there. Let there be space around this word and any sensations that come up for you. Are you afraid? Curious? Mystified? Whatever it is, just breathe into this moment and feel into your bodily sensations. Continue to sit with these sensations and remain as present as you can be to your direct experience, letting thought be thought, idea be idea, sensation be sensation. Breathe in and breathe out. After a set time of twenty to forty minutes, open your eyes and ring the bell to conclude the meditation.

———◆·◆———

The Buddha once taught that just as an elephant's footprint makes the largest impression on the earth, so too does meditating on impermanence make the largest impression on our mind. In other words, we have a lot to gain from contemplating death. I invite you to do this with me. Start with the question I posed back in January: *Who am I?* As you made your way through this book—reading, meditating, and writing—I sincerely hope you have reflected deeply on your experience of self. Who are you, really?

Just as your true nature is that which makes life possible, you are also that which makes death possible. Life and death are two aspects of one source in full cycle at all times. Most of the time we don't think about our inevitable death (sometimes actively so), but the fact of death is certain. *When* we die is uncertain—we simply can't know. The human body is fragile, and there are infinite and mysterious ways to die, just as there are infinite and mysterious ways to live. Only spiritual insight and connection can support us in this transformation. There is nothing physical we can take with us when we die. No friend or lover can accompany us on the actual journey, except, of course, in love and presence. However, whenever the end of this life arrives, we can depart with a sense of contribution and authentic connection: *I gave, I lived, I loved*. In this way, we can leave this body with a transformative experience of generosity, gratitude, and joy for the magical experience of life.

## Writing Exercise on Sanctuary

Here's the difficult exercise I alluded to. I want you to write about an experience you've had with death. Maybe it was a "near-death experience" of your own (like mine, tied to my dark "tree of enlightenment"), or maybe you've seen the death of a loved one. Perhaps it was the death of a pet or wild animal. Whatever death you choose, make sure it was something that made an impact on you, and describe the experience and any revelations or emotions you feel about it. Instead of naming the emotions directly, see if you can allow the details to evoke the emotions.

## Writing Exercise: Your Obituary

I was in a little bit of a distracted and even agitated state the other day when I ran into a new friend at the post office. Anna Douglas is one of the founding members of the Spirit Rock Teachers Council, a terrific teacher, and an all-around lovely presence. Something in the mail had me stirred up—a bill, a notice, a check that still hadn't arrived. But then I stepped outside and ran into Anna, just standing there in all her gracefully composed glory. She looked completely at peace and ease, and her face lit up with surprise when she saw me. I took a deep breath and smiled. Everything inside me moved to calm and sweetness, everything coalesced in presence.

Anna and I chatted about travel, the upcoming holidays, how grateful we felt for the glorious recent rains, and finally about a new "Year to Live" class she was teaching. Anna's class involves her students writing their obituaries. I found this to be a beautiful and brilliant idea, and so perfect to conclude what I have lovingly come to think of as my "death chapter." And so, with a bow to Anna, I invite you to write your own obituary.

I want you to do this mindfully and creatively. Tune into any fears or resistances that arise. Imagine you have a full page in the *New York Times* or whatever your favorite newspaper (or website) is, and that your obituary will be read by thousands. Or maybe you're simply writing a note before you die that will be left behind and read by the intimate few in your circle or community. Either way, write into the following prompts using the traditional language and style of an obituary, or reinvent the obituary form anew. Freewrite into these questions and see what arises:

1. How do you want to be remembered?

2. What are the true highlights of your life?

3. Who were the people who most inspired or influenced you?

4. What did you learn being embodied in this life that you want to share with others?

5. What held the most meaning for you in your days on this earth?

═━◆━═

# Afterword

From this moment forward, may your writing practice be your sanctuary. May it truly enrich the full depth and experience of your life. Writing as a path to awakening is an invitation and celebration—it's your ticket back to your creative brilliance. Writing and meditation are ultimately one sacred gesture, and simultaneously a singular profane act. Life is short. Time is fleeting and invented—it's only really ever *now*. You are the greatest invention ever and you are completely insignificant. Get over it. And get devoted. Activate your voice and surrender to the ensuing silence. Allow failure to be your handmaiden. Love is showing up fully with presence—open-hearted, raw, and vulnerable to the world; it's the only thing that matters. All writing and creativity originate here and now. Stop thinking about it and get to work. I believe in you. You can do this! The universe and I have got your back.

# About the Author

Albert Flynn DeSilver is an American poet, memoirist, novelist, speaker, and workshop leader. He received a BFA in photography from the University of Colorado in 1991 and an MFA in new genres from the San Francisco Art Institute in 1995. Albert served as Marin County, California's first poet laureate from 2008 to 2010. His work has appeared in more than one hundred literary journals worldwide, including *ZYZZYVA*, *New American Writing*, *Hanging Loose*, *Jubilat*, *Exquisite Corpse*, *Jacket* (Australia), *Poetry Kanto* (Japan), and *Van Gogh's Ear* (France). He is the author of several books of poetry, including *Letters to Early Street* (La Alameda/University of New Mexico Press, 2007) and *Walking Tooth & Cloud* (French Connection Press–Paris, 2008), as well as the memoir *Beamish Boy*, which Kirkus Reviews calls "a beautifully written memoir of awakening and self-acceptance." *Writing as a Path to Awakening* is based on the popular writing workshops by the same name taught nationally by Albert at The Omega Institute, The Esalen Institute, Spirit Rock Meditation Center, and writing conferences nationally.

Albert's latest retreat schedule—as well as tips and resources on meditation and writing—can be found at albertflynndesilver.com. He lives in Northern California.

# About Sounds True

Sounds True is a multimedia publisher whose mission is to inspire and support personal transformation and spiritual awakening. Founded in 1985 and located in Boulder, Colorado, we work with many of the leading spiritual teachers, thinkers, healers, and visionary artists of our time. We strive with every title to preserve the essential "living wisdom" of the author or artist. It is our goal to create products that not only provide information to a reader or listener, but that also embody the quality of a wisdom transmission.

For those seeking genuine transformation, Sounds True is your trusted partner. At SoundsTrue.com you will find a wealth of free resources to support your journey, including exclusive weekly audio interviews, free downloads, interactive learning tools, and other special savings on all our titles.

To learn more, please visit SoundsTrue.com/freegifts or call us toll-free at 800.333.9185.

**SOUNDS TRUE**
many voices, one journey